WHOLE GRAINS FOR BUSY PEOPLE

OTHER BOOKS BY LORNA SASS

Whole Grains Every Day, Every Way

Pressure Perfect

The New Vegan Cookbook

The Pressured Cook: Over 75 One-Pot Meals in Minutes

The New Soy Cookbook

Lorna Sass' Short-Cut Vegetarian

Great Vegetarian Cooking Under Pressure

Lorna Sass' Complete Vegetarian Kitchen
(formerly titled Recipes from an Ecological Kitchen)

Cooking Under Pressure

In Search of the Perfect Meal: A Collection of the Best Food Writings
of Roy Andries de Groot (selected and edited)

Christmas Feasts from History

Dinner with Tom Jones

To the Queen's Taste: Elizabethan Feasts and Recipes

To the King's Taste: Richard II's Book of Feasts and Recipes

WHOLE GRAINS
FOR BUSY
PEOPLE

FAST, FLAVOR-PACKED MEALS AND MORE FOR EVERYONE

LORNA SASS

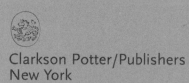

Clarkson Potter/Publishers
New York

Library of Congress Cataloging-in-Publication Data
Sass, Lorna J.
    Whole grains for busy people / Lorna Sass. — 1st ed.
        p.   cm.
    Includes index.
    1. Cookery (Cereals)   2. Grain.   I. Title.
    TX808.S273   2009
    641.6'31—dc22   2008016593

ISBN 978-0-307-40782-5

Printed in the United States of America

Design by Maggie Hinders

10 9 8 7 6 5 4 3 2 1

First Edition

For Michael

The song is you

contents

introduction

Congratulations!

YOU HAVE PICKED UP THIS BOOK because you are a busy person who wants to incorporate more whole grains into your diet. No doubt you've heard about the health-promoting benefits of whole grains but may feel confused about selecting the best products in the supermarket. You may also be wondering how you will find the time to learn about cooking new foods when your schedule is already packed.

I wrote this book for you—and for me, too.

I'm also busy, and truth be told, I'm an impatient cook. When I get hungry, watch out:

I want my dinner ready in a flash.

I want to eat tasty, healthy food.

I don't want to wash more than one pot after dinner.

So, for a follow-up to my award-winning *Whole Grains Every Day, Every Way*, I challenged myself to experiment exclusively with whole grains that cook in under 30 minutes. I also challenged myself to cook as many meals as possible in only one pot.

These challenges led me to try many of the new whole-grain products now in the marketplace, from brown rice pasta to quick-cooking barley. As you know, the choices can be dizzying, and it soon became my added mission to separate the whole wheat from the chaff.

Once I selected the best ingredients, I created dozens of main-dish soups, stews, salads, and skillet suppers that you can have on the table quickly—most in a half hour or less. And I couldn't resist whipping up some homemade mixes to have at the ready for easily creating whole-grain muffins, mini-loaves, scones, pie crusts, crumbles, and cookies.

The results of my experiments are the flavor-packed, kid-friendly recipes you'll find in this volume. After trying them, I hope you'll agree that introducing more whole grains into your diet is easy, tasty, and fun.

Happy cooking!

LORNA SASS

the
busy cook's
guide to
whole
grains

WHY EAT WHOLE GRAINS?

When the bran and germ are stripped away from a whole grain to produce white flour or white rice, 50 to 90 percent of the nutrients and phytochemicals are lost, depending upon the grain.

So why, you may wonder, did we start eating refined grains in the first place? The reason is simple: once the protective bran layer and the oil-rich germ are removed, grains and the flour ground from them remain shelf stable and last indefinitely. This stability is profitable for suppliers and grocers and convenient for us. We've all gotten used to having white rice and refined pasta on our pantry shelves for years. They cook quickly and are pleasing to eat, so why bother making a change?

Because each part of the grain contributes different nutrients, scientists believe that eating all parts of the grain together is critical to disease prevention. Studies over the past decade have shown that people who consume at least three servings of whole grains per day reduce their risk of stroke, obesity, heart disease, diabetes, and cancers related to the digestive system. Some studies have even concluded that whole grains are often a better source of disease-fighting phytochemicals and antioxidants than fruits and vegetables!

In addition to providing essential nutrients, disease-fighting antioxidants, and health-promoting fiber, whole grains are absorbed by our bodies more slowly than refined grains. Since slower absorption prevents spikes in sugar and insulin, eating three servings of whole grains daily can reduce the onset of diabetes and metabolic syndrome. (To stay abreast of current research on whole grains and health, visit www.wholegrainscouncil.org.)

Science and health aside, a fine reason to eat whole grains is that they taste so good! And now, with all of the quick-cooking grains and whole-grain products so readily available, it's never been easier to eat delicious foods that also happen to be good for us.

What Is a Whole Grain?

Grains are edible members of the grass family of plants. Among the most common grains are wheat, barley, oats, corn (including popcorn!), rice, and rye.

Whole grains have three edible parts: the bran, the germ, and the endosperm. Each part of the grain contains essential nutrients and performs a vital function for the plant and for us when we eat it.

Take a kernel of wheat, for example. The bran is the hard, brownish layers of skin that protect the germ and endosperm from insects and disease. For us, the bran layers are a concentrated source of fiber, B vitamins, and trace minerals.

The tiny germ lies just below the bran at one end of the kernel. Although it accounts for only about 2 percent of the dry grain's weight, it is the life source of the grain. For us, it provides vitamins B and E, essential fatty acids, trace minerals, phytochemicals, and unsaturated lipids.

The endosperm, or starchy center of the grain, supplies food to the growing seedling. Over 50 percent of the endosperm is starch and about 10 percent is plant protein. The endosperm contains relatively few vitamins, minerals, and phyto-chemicals and hardly any fiber. To the plant and to us, it provides quick energy in the form of simple carbohydrates.

What's Fiber and Why Does It Matter?

Fiber is the part of plant foods that the body can't digest. There are two types of fiber and each plays an important role. Soluble fiber dissolves in water and forms a gel that absorbs LDL (bad cholesterol) and eliminates it from the system, thereby promoting heart health. Insoluble fiber acts like a broom, sweeping out waste as it moves along, thereby improving digestion. Both forms of fiber create a sense of being full—an amazing phenomenon since fiber has no calories. Because eating whole grains results in this feeling of satiety, many people find it easier to lose weight when they add whole grains to their diets.

Is It Hard Going from White to Brown?

The resounding answer is no.

Try these few easy steps to begin:

• Buy bread that is at least 50 percent whole grain. Once you and your family are used to that, try bread made of 100 percent whole grain.

• Buy whole-wheat pita. You probably won't even notice the difference.

• Switch to a whole-grain breakfast cereal, or start by mixing a whole-grain cereal with your current favorite. Or try having instant oatmeal for breakfast.

• Opt for corn or whole-wheat tortillas over white flour ones.

• Try whole-grain crackers, some of which—like Triscuits—have been whole grain all along.

• Try brown rice or whole-wheat pasta—or start off with a pasta that's made partially of whole wheat—instead of a classic refined wheat pasta. (By the way, farro and other whole-grain pastas are becoming more popular, even in Italy!)

IDENTIFYING WHOLE-GRAIN PRODUCTS

The easiest way to identify whole-grain products is to look at the label and make sure that "whole" is the first word listed: for example, "whole wheat." Since ingredients are listed in order of weight, this will tell you that the product contains a significant amount of whole-grain wheat.

A growing number of products now sport the Whole Grain Stamp, an initiative of the Whole Grains Council. Make sure that the stamp has the "100%" banner across the middle and you'll know that 100 percent of the grain is whole grain. You'll also be assured that each serving of the product is equivalent to one full serving of whole grains. (See What's a Serving Size? on page 14.)

If there is no stamp on the package, check the amount of fiber per serving. For example, a slice of whole-grain bread will have at least 3 grams of fiber, while a slice of bread made primarily of white flour will have only 1 gram or less.

Manufacturers often use numerous misleading phrases to suggest the inclusion of whole grains. Don't let yourself be fooled by any of the following:

"MADE WITH WHOLE GRAIN." Okay, maybe there are a few teaspoons of whole grains in the mix, but the majority of the flour is likely to be refined.

"100% WHEAT" is a particularly deceptive phrase. All it means is that the only type of flour in the product is wheat flour, not necessarily whole-wheat flour.

"MULTIGRAIN" means that there is more than one type of grain included but, again, is no guarantee that any of them is whole.

"STONE GROUND" refers to grains coarsely ground in a stone mill, but you still need to see if the first word on the label is "whole." For example, many stone-ground cornmeals are made from degerminated corn kernels.

Don't be tricked by a dark color, which can be caused by the inclusion of molasses or food coloring. On the contrary, keep in mind that some whole-grain foods, such as oats and white wheat, can have a light color.

In short, the only way to be sure you are purchasing a product containing 100 percent whole grains is to see the word "whole" in front of the name of each grain mentioned in the label.

What's a Serving Size?

One serving of whole grains weighs in at 1 ounce. The 2005 Dietary Guidelines for Americans suggests that adults eat at least 3 ounces of whole grains per day.

Here are the equivalents to 1 serving size (1 ounce) of some popular 100 percent whole-grain foods:

BAGEL = ½ bagel	CRACKERS = 5 to 7 small
BREAD = 1 slice	PASTA = ½ cup cooked
BROWN RICE = ½ cup cooked	POPCORN = 2 cups
CEREAL = ½ cup cooked	TORTILLAS = 1 small

QUICK-COOKING WHOLE GRAINS

If you have the impression that all whole grains take a long time to cook, I have good news to share. First, highly nutritious whole grains like quinoa, buckwheat, and millet take only 15 minutes to a half hour to become tender. Second, when whole grains are steam-rolled and flattened into flakes—like old-fashioned oats—they take only about 5 minutes to cook. Third, numerous whole grains like brown and wild rice are now available in quick-cooking form. Lastly, cooked heat-and-eat brown and wild rices are available frozen and vacuum-packed.

Supermarkets of all kinds, including Trader Joe's and Whole Foods, now stock a variety of whole grains in various forms, thanks to the growing number of consumers requesting them. The recipes in this book rely almost entirely on the quick-cooking whole grains shelved in the rice or breakfast cereal aisles. If you can't find what you need there, head to Amazon.com, which sells just about everything these days. Then request that your supermarket get hip and stock these items if they don't want to continue losing your business!

Selection and Storage

When buying packaged grains, look for the expiration date, and buy the one with the latest date. When purchasing from a bulk bin, sniff to be sure that the grains have either a faintly sweet aroma or no aroma at all.

Keep in mind that some of the whole-grain products you'll be purchasing contain the oil-rich germ and should be stored in a cool environment to avoid rancidity. While some whole grains are more stable than others and can be stored in the pantry—oatmeal, for example—as a general rule it's best to refrigerate or freeze all whole grains and to refrigerate all whole-grain products, including pasta.

To Rinse or Not to Rinse

I rarely rinse grains before cooking them. Most grains packaged in this country are clean and ready to go. If you purchase grains from a bulk bin or the grains in your package look dusty, rinse and drain them well.

About the Grains

In the following pages you'll find descriptions of the quick-cooking grains called for in the recipes. Check the chart on pages 20–21 for information about where these grains can be purchased; the vast majority are available in supermarkets but a few require a trip to a health-food store. And, of course, just about everything these days can be ordered online. (For information on whole-grain products—including pastas, pitas, pizza crusts, and tortillas—see pages 20–21, 26–27, and 29. Background on whole-grain flours can be found starting on page 30.) For the convenience of those who are gluten-intolerant (see page 31), I've labeled the grains that are gluten-free with the abbreviation GF.

BARLEY, FLAKES: Made from pearl barley that has been steam-rolled and pressed in a process similar to that of making oatmeal, these cook in 10 to 15 minutes. For more on barley in general, see Barley, quick-cooking, below.

BARLEY, QUICK-COOKING: This parboiled product takes only 10 minutes to cook. It is made from pearl barley, meaning that all of the germ and much of the bran have been rubbed off. Even though quick-cooking barley is not a whole grain, I have included it in this book because even after processing, it contains an impressive 5 grams each of dietary fiber and protein per ½ cup cooked serving. Barley is also a good source of niacin and phosphorous and, like oats, contains beta glucans that have been shown to help lower total cholesterol levels and the risk of coronary heart disease.
NOTE: Quick-cooking barley and barley flakes cannot be used interchangeably.

BUCKWHEAT, TOASTED (ALSO KNOWN AS KASHA) AND UNTOASTED GROATS (GF): Although its name suggests otherwise, buckwheat is not related botanically to wheat. In fact, it's not a cereal grass at all. Rather, buckwheat is a flowering plant related to rhubarb that has a nutritional profile similar to grains. It is a good source of protein (especially lysine, which is relatively uncommon in cereal grains) and a fine source of minerals, including iron, phosphorus, and potassium as well as vitamins B and E.

Buckwheat is naturally quick-cooking, taking only about 15 minutes to become tender. Once the inedible black hull of this charming pyramidal grain is removed, the grain is often toasted to create dark, earthy-tasting kasha. Light whole buckwheat groats are untoasted and have a mild flavor. Dark and light buckwheat can be used interchangeably.

If the grains are not coated with either egg or oil and cooked in a limited amount of liquid, they quickly collapse into a porridge.

BUCKWHEAT, GRANULATED (GF): Light (untoasted) buckwheat groats that have been finely ground, granulated buckwheat makes a good breakfast cereal and polenta-like side dish.

BULGUR, COARSE AND FINE: Bulgur is made by first cooking whole kernels of wheat in water. The kernels are then dried and ground into bits of various sizes—an ancient method of creating fast food and preserving it at the same time. The ground bulgur is sifted to separate the various sizes. The largest grind is called coarse bulgur and requires about 20 minutes of cooking—unlike the fine grinds, which require only brief soaking. Although some bran is lost in processing, bulgur still has more than twice as much fiber as brown rice and is also a good source of iron, magnesium, and niacin. Look for bulgur that is a rich caramel-brown color; light bulgur may be prepared from refined wheat stripped of bran. Don't confuse bulgur with cracked wheat, which is not precooked.

COUSCOUS, WHOLE WHEAT: Although normally thought of as a grain, couscous is actually tiny, pellet-sized pasta made of whole-grain wheat flour (usually durum) and water. Whole-grain couscous requires only brief soaking in just-boiled water. To prevent the grains from sticking together, coat them lightly with oil before steeping. For a more flavorful dish, soak the couscous in broth rather than water. The amounts of protein and dietary fiber vary considerably from brand to brand. Among the highest in both is Fantastic World Foods; ½ cup of its uncooked couscous contains 7 grams of protein and 6 grains of dietary fiber.
NOTE: The recommended ratio of water to dry couscous differs among brands; the recipes will remind you to check package instructions.

FARRO: An ancient cousin of wheat that has a faintly sweet taste and pleasingly chewy texture. Most farro is imported from Italy and partially pearled ("semi-perlato"), meaning that some of the bran has been removed, speeding up the cooking time to about 20 minutes. Half a cup of cooked farro contains approximately 7 grams of protein. Unlike many grains, cooked farro does not become hard when refrigerated, making it an especially good choice for grain salads that you'd like to prepare in advance. Farro releases a creamy starch when cooked in ample liquid, making a pleasing risotto.

HOMINY (GF): A type of large-kernel dried corn that has been cooked in a solution containing either lime or lye. These alkali ingredients cause the tough outer hulls to loosen, so that they can be rubbed off and washed away, leaving the chewy, starchy center. This process, known to the ancient Mayans and Aztecs, makes the niacin in the kernels bioavailable to humans. A cup of canned, white hominy has 4 grams of fiber, 1 microgram of iron, and 5 micrograms of choline, a nutrient in the vitamin B family. Yellow hominy has slightly less iron and no choline. (Since the hominy grits sold in supermarkets have less than half the fiber of whole hominy, I do not use grits in the recipes.)

Hominy cooked from scratch is delicious but takes hours to prepare, so I've called for canned hominy. "Posole" is both the Spanish name for this grain and the name of a slow-cooked stew made with hominy and pork.

MILLET, WHOLE AND GRITS (GF): Sometimes labeled "hulled millet," referring to the fact that the inedible hull has been removed, millet is a very nutritious grain, rich in protein and a good source of phosphorus and potassium. The grain looks like small, straw-yellow beads and cooks in about 25 minutes. Toasting it before adding water deepens millet's mild flavor. Depending upon the amount of water used, it can either be made into a fluffy pilaf or a breakfast porridge. Millet cooks unevenly, so there is always some variation in texture. Some batches taste slightly bitter, so it's a good idea to combine millet with assertively flavored ingredients. (The bitterness disappears after the cooked millet sits for a while.)

The advantage to cracking millet into grits is that it brings the cooking time down to 15 minutes. All of the millet recipes in this book use cracked millet, which is also called millet grits. You can purchase cracked millet, but it will go rancid more quickly than whole millet, so it's best to grind millet as needed—easily done by pulsing the grains in a spice grinder. Cracked millet is good for polenta-like dishes and breakfast porridge.

OATMEAL (ROLLED OLD-FASHIONED OATS) (SOME BRANDS GF): Oatmeal is made by pressing and rolling whole or steel-cut oats into flakes. The thinner the oats are rolled, the faster the flakes cook. Instant oats are the thinnest and practically dissolve upon contact with hot liquid. (Do not substitute instant oatmeal in the recipes; it has little to no texture.) All forms of oats are considered whole grains.

Like barley, oats contain a soluble fiber called beta-glucan, which gives oats their smooth, silky texture. On the health front, beta-glucan has been shown to lower both total cholesterol and LDL (bad cholesterol).

Oats are gluten-free, but they are often contaminated with wheat either in the fields or during processing. Those on gluten-free diets have to make certain of the purity of any particular brand. (Bob's Red Mill is one company that sells guaranteed GF oats.)

OATS, STEEL-CUT (SOME BRANDS GF): Made by cutting whole groats into bits with steel blades.

POPCORN (GF): Arguably the best known and most popular whole grain in America, popcorn is made from varieties of flint and dent corn that have a high moisture content and hard hulls. When heated, the internal moisture develops into steam. As the steam pressure builds, it forces the kernels to burst open. Although popcorn comes in colors, don't be fooled: once it's popped, it all looks the same. As everyone knows, popcorn makes a great snack unless it's loaded with butter (or even worse, fake fat that tastes like butter). One cup of popped popcorn without added oil has only 31 calories and offers 1 gram each of protein and fiber. Try grinding popped popcorn in a spice grinder to make a delicious crisp coating for turkey (see recipe, page 78) that contains more fiber and nutrition than a standard white bread–crumb treatment.

QUINOA, FLAKES (GF): Quinoa grains that are steamed and roller-pressed, these tiny "snowflakes" reconstitute within a minute. They are great for making quick soups and creamy polenta-like side dishes.

QUINOA, WHOLE (GF): A small, versatile grain from the Andes that cooks in under 15 minutes, quinoa is not a true grain; it is actually a seed related to the pigweed family. Beige/tan quinoa is the tastiest; substitute less-flavorful red quinoa in small amounts if you'd like to add color. Quinoa contains all of the essential amino acids, making it an excellent source of complete protein—8 grams per cooked cup. When choosing among brands, choose the one with the highest fiber, indicating that minimal bran has been rubbed off during cleaning. An excellent choice is Bob's Red Mill, which is cleaned by thorough washing rather than abrasion, so no bran is lost.

(continued on page 22)

Quick-Cooking Grains at a Glance

GRAIN	BRAND(S)	AVAILABILITY	COMMENTS
BARLEY, flakes	King Arthur Neshaminy Valley	Mail-order Health-food stores	Cannot be used interchangeably with quick-cooking barley
BARLEY, quick-cooking	Mother's (a division of Quaker/Pepsi)	Supermarkets (rice and grains aisle)	Cannot be used interchangeably with barley flakes
BUCKWHEAT, toasted (kasha) (GF)		Supermarkets; health-food stores	Toasted whole buckwheat groats; earthy flavor
BUCKWHEAT, untoasted (GF)	Bob's Red Mill and many others	Health-food stores; mail order	Same nutrients as toasted but considerably milder taste
BUCKWHEAT, granulated (GF)	Pocono (Birkett Mills)	Supermarkets (breakfast aisle)	Also called Cream of Buckwheat; quick-cooking breakfast cereal or polenta-like side dish
BULGUR, coarse	Goya Sunnyland Mills	Supermarkets (rice aisle) Mail order	Good for pilafs; requires cooking
BULGUR, fine	Sunnyland Mills	Middle Eastern stores; mail order	Rehydrate by steeping in just-boiled water
COUSCOUS, whole wheat	Many brands	Supermarkets (rice aisle); health-food stores	Minuscule pasta; great for quick side-dish pilafs and salads
FARRO	Roland	Many supermarkets; gourmet shops	Imported farro is semi-pearled
HOMINY (canned) (GF)	Goya	Supermarkets (bean aisle)	Rinse before using
MILLET, whole (GF)	Bob's Red Mill and many other brands	Health-food stores	
MILLET, grits (GF)		Health-food stores	Grind from whole millet in a spice grinder
OATMEAL (rolled oats)	Quaker and many organic brands	Supermarkets; health-food stores	

GF = GLUTEN-FREE

Quick-Cooking Grains at a Glance

GRAIN	BRAND(S)	AVAILABILITY	COMMENTS
POPCORN (GF)		Supermarkets; health-food stores	Check labels to avoid trans fats and less healthy oils
QUINOA, flakes (GF)	Ancient Harvest	Health-food stores (near breakfast cereals)	
QUINOA, whole (GF)	Bob's Red Mill	Supermarkets; health-food stores	When there's choice, select brand with highest fiber content
RICE, brown, fully cooked (GF)	Trader Joe's Kraft Success Rice Expressions	Trader Joe's Supermarkets Supermarkets (organic aisle)	Heat-and-eat; both frozen and shelf-stable available Shelf stable; sold in microwavable cups Shelf stable; sold in microwavable pouches
RICE, brown Minute (GF)	Kraft Foods	Supermarkets	Look for Minute instant whole-grain brown rice; not inter-changeable with Uncle Ben's
RICE, Chinese black (GF)	Lotus Foods	Gourmet shops; some supermarkets; online	Can be used interchangeably with Thai black rice in the recipes in this book
RICE, Thai black sticky (GF)		Asian groceries; online	Can be used interchangeably with Chinese black rice in the recipes in this book
RYE, flakes	Many brands	Health-food stores	
WILD RICE, fully cooked (GF)	Trader Joe's	Trader Joe's	Heat-and-eat; sold in shelf-stable pouches
WILD RICE, instant (GF)	Haddon-House Reese	Supermarkets Supermarkets	Can be hard to find
WILD RICE, quick-cooking (GF)	Lundberg	Supermarkets; health-food stores	Takes 15 minutes longer to cook than instant; sold in shelf-stable pouches

RICE, BROWN, FULLY COOKED: This ready-to-eat whole-grain product is available in two forms: microwavable, shelf-stable cups and frozen. I like the texture of the frozen cooked rice better than the shelf-stable cups.

RICE, BROWN MINUTE (GF): This Kraft Foods precooked product has approximately the same nutritional profile as cooked-from-scratch long-grain brown rice—3 grams of protein and 2 grams of fiber per ⅔ cup cooked—but the dramatically reduced cooking time of 10 minutes rather than 45. The flavor and texture are considerably improved by toasting the rice before cooking and using less water than suggested on the package, which is what I've advised in all of the recipes calling for this product. Because this rice is partially cooked, it requires less water and has a lower yield than traditionally cooked brown rice. For example, 1 cup of Minute rice requires ¾ cup of water and yields 1½ cups of cooked rice.
NOTE: The recipes in this book do not work with Uncle Ben's Instant Brown Rice, which has different cooking requirements.

RICE, CHINESE BLACK: A delicious, slightly sweet rice, this organic black grain is imported from China and distributed under the trademarked name Forbidden Black Rice by Lotus Foods. It cooks in about 30 minutes. This heirloom rice is stunning: black when raw and burgundy when cooked. Two-thirds cup of cooked black rice contains approximately 5 grams of protein and 2 grams of fiber. It can be used interchangeably with Thai sticky black rice in the recipes in this book.

RICE, THAI BLACK STICKY: A striking, slightly sweet rice imported from Thailand, this grain cooks in about 25 minutes. It can be used interchangeably with Chinese black rice in the recipes in this book.

RYE, FLAKES: Rye flakes are made by pressing the whole kernel through rollers to flatten them.

WILD RICE, INSTANT, QUICK-COOKING, AND FULLY COOKED: Despite its name, wild rice is neither a rice nor a whole grain, but it is commonly lumped with whole grains because of its impressive nutritional profile. Actually an aquatic grass, wild rice contains more protein than brown rice and is also a good source of lysine and fiber. The cooking time of wild rice is wildly unpredictable, but instant wild rice is parboiled and reliably cooks in 10 minutes. Haddon House is the only brand I've seen in supermarkets, and it can be difficult to locate in some parts of the country. Another brand to look for is Reese Quick-Cooking Minnesota Wild Rice. Lundberg sells pouches of shelf-stable, precooked wild rice that cooks in 25 minutes; if you use it instead, adjust the recipe timing accordingly. Fully cooked, ready to eat wild rice is available in shelf-stable pouches.

The Ten Quickest Recipes

While all of the recipes aim to make it possible for you to get a healthy main course on the table in about a half hour, try one of the following recipes when you're feeling especially rushed.

10-Minute Quinoa Soup with Avocado and Corn (page 43)

Hominy and Kidney Bean Chili (page 51)

Michael's Quick Brown Rice with Tuna and Green Beans (page 79)

Quinoa-Crusted Chicken Cutlets with Cilantro Pesto (page 76)

Soft Chicken Tacos with Smoked Paprika Sour Cream (page 80)

Skillet Macaroni and Cheese with Ham and Spinach (page 87)

Aztec Couscous Salad (page 134)

Anything Goes Pizza (page 122)

Fusilli with Zucchini Ribbons and Pesto (page 90)

Steamed Mussels with Garlicky Brown Rice and White Beans (page 54)

WHOLE-GRAIN PASTAS

Do you like the idea of eating pasta that contains fewer calories but a whopping 25 percent more protein and three times the amount of fiber than regular durum wheat products? If so, consider stocking your pantry with 100 percent whole-grain pastas.

If you tried whole-wheat or another type of whole-grain pasta a few years ago and were disappointed by the gummy, gritty, or mushy experience, I'd like to encourage you to give the category another chance. The technology for manufacturing whole-grain pastas has improved dramatically. In fact, many pastas now lining the supermarket shelves and boldly proclaiming themselves to be whole-grain taste very much like the pasta we know and love.

If you prefer a slow transition, consider beginning with a blended pasta. Brands such as Barilla Plus and Ronzoni Healthy Harvest contain whole wheat mixed with other ingredients, such as refined wheat flour or ground legumes and flax. These pastas have been blended to create the mouth feel of traditional pasta while improving the nutritional value considerably—the legumes and flax boost the protein levels and add omega 3s.

Many brands now offer the toothsome texture and mild, sweet taste of the traditional, refined durum wheat pastas. Not surprisingly, many of the best whole-wheat pastas are now imported from Italy, including the Whole Foods 365 brand and Trader Joe's—oops! I mean Trader Giotto's.

One of the great discoveries I made while writing this book is brown rice pasta. You'll often find this pasta in the section devoted to gluten-free products, and indeed, it was probably developed to meet the needs of people who can't digest the gluten in wheat.

The taste and texture of brown rice pasta was so appealing to me that I began experimenting with quick ways to prepare it. I had surprising success cooking the pasta and sauce together in a large sauté pan, using a technique called skillet pasta by *Cook's Illustrated,* where I first read about it. Unlike most other whole-grain pastas, brown rice pasta doesn't overcook in a flash, providing a few extra minutes, if needed, for the sauce and other ingredients to complete cooking.

I had so much fun with skillet pastas that I went a little crazy developing recipes for just about every shape available—and there are many. It's certainly a boon to avoid the 15-minute waiting time for a big pot of water to come to a boil, but perhaps a better reason for cooking pasta in limited water is that the silken starch it releases becomes part of the sauce. And there's only one pot to clean!

Here are a few tips to ensure success when preparing any whole-grain pasta:

- For a more distinct nutty, wheaty flavor, cook the pasta in salted water. If you prefer a milder taste, omit the salt.
- Consider package timing a rule of thumb. It is frequently wrong! Set your timer for 6 minutes less than the recommended minimum cooking time, and begin tasting at that point. If you aren't sure if the pasta is done, cut a piece in half and see if it is one color throughout. If you spot any opaque areas, continue cooking.
- If you like your pasta al dente, drain it when it is ever-so-slightly undercooked. The pasta will continue cooking in its own residual heat, and you will avoid the risk of overcooking.

I recommend using only brown rice pasta when making skillet pastas. Other types of whole-grain pastas don't fare well using this technique; they often cook unevenly, become too soft, and in some instances, actually fall apart.

The chart that follows lists some brands you'll enjoy. It's also worth trying your supermarket's house brand. The ShopRite whole-wheat pasta I bought was well priced and quite pleasant.

Whole-Grain Pastas at a Glance

TYPE	BRAND	AVAILABILITY	SHAPES	COMMENTS
BROWN RICE, 100% (GF)	Tinkyada	Supermarkets (gluten-free section); health-food stores	About a dozen different shapes, including lasagne noodles	Terrific taste and texture; some shapes organic
	Lundberg	Health-food stores; some supermarkets (gluten-free aisle)	Penne, rotini, spaghetti	Organic
	Trader Joe's	Trader Joe's	Numerous, including penne and spaghetti	Looks and tastes the same as Tinkyada; some shapes organic
BUCKWHEAT SOBA, 100% (GF)	Many imported brands from Japan	Asian groceries; some supermarkets	Thin, round, long noodles	
BUCKWHEAT SOBA, blended	Eden Foods	Health-food stores; some supermarkets		Organic, makes both 100% and blended with whole wheat
FARRO, 100%	Rustichella d'Abruzzo	Gourmet shops; online	Spaghetti, fettucine, orzo	Pricey, but a real treat with distinct "wheaty" nuttiness
KAMUT®	Eden Foods	Health-food stores	Udon	Organic; Kamut is an unhybridized relative of wheat
QUINOA, blended (GF)	Ancient Harvest	Supermarkets; health-food stores	Spaghetti and numerous cut pastas	Blended with corn flour
	Go-Go	Health-food stores; mail order (gluten-free sources)	Spaghetti and fusilli	Organic, blended with rice flour
SPELT	Vita-Spelt	Health-food stores	Many, including angel hair and lasagne	Spelt is a relatively unhybridized relative of wheat

GF = GLUTEN-FREE

Whole-Grain Pastas at a Glance

TYPE	BRAND	AVAILABILITY	SHAPES	COMMENTS
WHOLE WHEAT, 100%	DeCecco	Supermarkets	Spaghetti	Toothsome; good "wheaty" flavor
	Del Verde	Supermarkets	Spaghetti, fusilli	Smooth texture, chewy, light wheat flavor
	Hodgson Mill	Many supermarkets; health-food stores	Spaghetti, fettucine, and many cut shapes	Good texture with mild wheat flavor; organic varieties containing ground flax seed are less toothsome and more fragile
	Trader Joe's	Trader Joe's		Organic; appealing "wheaty" taste; varieties containing ground flax seed also recommended; varieties based on sprouted wheat disappointing
	Whole Foods 365 Everyday Value	Whole Foods Markets	Spaghetti, penne, shells, etc.	Organic; hearty flavor and good texture for a good price
WHOLE WHEAT, 50% or more	Barilla	Supermarkets		Blended with other grains and legumes; firm texture and light wheat flavor similar to refined pasta
	Ronzoni Healthy Harvest	Supermarkets	Spaghetti	Blended pasta with added bran; good texture but no flavor

FLATBREADS: PITA, PIZZA, AND TORTILLAS

It's a great boon for the busy cook to have a freezer full of flatbreads for impromptu meals and snacks. Fortunately, the shelves are now full of whole-grain choices in this category.

PITA: Whole-wheat pita bread is now available in most supermarkets. Try to find a brand that has a short list of ingredients, namely, whole-wheat flour, water, yeast, and perhaps salt. Many brands use half enriched refined flour and add preservatives to retard spoilage. If these are the only ones available, they still make a good start, with about 3 grams of dietary fiber and 5 grams of protein.

In addition to stuffing it for sandwiches, pita can be transformed into crisp, seasoned chips: Halve the pita horizontally and spray the insides with olive oil. Dust with a seasoning, such as smoked Spanish paprika or curry powder. Bake at 350°F— I do this in my toaster oven—until curled up and crisp, 3 to 4 minutes (longer in a conventional oven). Break into pieces. Pita chips are delicious with guacamole and also make nice croutonlike toppings for soups.

PIZZA: Whole-grain pizza crusts aren't as easy to find as whole-grain pita, but they are becoming increasingly available. If you can't buy a standard whole-wheat crust in your supermarket, set two whole-grain burrito wraps on a cookie sheet and take it from there—or make mini-pizzas on pita bread.

Making pizza at home is a tasty way to use up leftovers since you can use just about anything for the topping. See the recipe for pizza on page 120 and the box on page 123 for some topping ideas.

TORTILLAS: It's fun and easy to get a serving of whole grains by using a whole-grain wrap, but beware the products that come in colors other than shades of beige and brown. It's fine if the dough includes spinach or tomato, but often such colors and flavors distract consumers from the fact that the tortillas are not made from organic flour and contain unnecessary ingredients like trans fats, sugar, corn syrup, and preservatives. Take a good look at the label. Ideally the first ingredient should be some type of whole-grain flour. A tortilla made entirely of whole wheat will contain 5 grams each of fiber and protein.

In addition to using tortillas for wraps, I like to use them instead of lasagne noodles to prepare quick, layered casseroles. They are also great for making enchiladas, burritos, and quesadillas. Check out the recipes on pages 125 and 128.

Flatbreads at a Glance

TYPE	BRAND	AVAILABILITY	COMMENTS
PITA, whole wheat	Many local brands	Supermarkets; health-food stores	Try to find those made only of whole-wheat flour, water, and yeast
PIZZA CRUST, whole wheat	Trader Giotto's	Trader Joe's	Whole-wheat and a blend of other whole-grain flours; includes soy
TORTILLAS, corn (some brands GF)	Food for Life	Health-food stores/freezer	Made from sprouted, organic, whole-kernel corn
	Sonoma	Hard to find whole grain; look in frozen section of health-food stores	Stone ground, organic
	Trader Joe's	Trader Joe's	Made from freshly ground corn; mild taste
TORTILLAS, whole wheat	Garden of Eatin'	Supermarkets; health-food stores	Nice "wheaty" flavor
	Whole Foods	Whole Foods	Nice "wheaty" flavor
	French Meadow Bakery	Health-food stores	A variety of organic tortillas based on whole wheat blended with other grain and bean flours
	Trader Jose's	Trader Joe's	Whole-grain wheat blended with other flours and flax; also whole wheat blended with sunflower oil and honey

GF = GLUTEN-FREE

WHOLE-GRAIN FLOURS

It's obvious that whole-grain flours are ground from the whole grain, but it's less known that their nutritional values are affected by how the grains are milled.

There are several reasons to opt for stone-ground whole-grain flours when they are available. First, when whole kernels are crushed between two flat millstones, the bran and germ get fairly evenly distributed into the flour. Second, stone-grinding produces less heat than other milling methods, thereby preserving more of the flavor and nutritional value of the grains. Third, the slightly larger size of stone-ground flour particles results in flour that is digested more slowly, keeping blood sugar levels stable and providing a steady stream of energy.

Selecting and Storing

When possible, opt for products labeled "100% stone-ground." You are more likely to find these in health-food stores or by mail order than in supermarkets. When buying whole-grain flour in the supermarket, make sure that the label lists the whole grain as the first and, ideally, only ingredient.

Because grinding exposes the oil-rich germ, flour becomes rancid much more quickly than the whole grains themselves. Always check the expiration date and buy the package that is

Grinding Your Own Flour

It's very easy to grind small amounts of some grains in a spice grinder. Buckwheat groats, for example, are soft enough to grind into flour as needed. In the case of harder grains, like wheat, oats, and barley, you can buy flakes and grind them into flour in small batches.

I have had two little Krups electric coffee grinders for years, one of which is reserved for grinding grains and spices, and it's never let me down. For even grinding, shake the grinder gently as you process the grains. (Some people prefer using a blender for this purpose, but I have never found a blender that has lived up to its promise, except for the Vita-Mix, which is in a class all by itself and commands the price tag to match.)

freshest. If feasible, purchase flour in small amounts. Always refrigerate or freeze it in a well-sealed container, and try to use it within 3 months.

Wheat and Non-Wheat Flours

The main difference between wheat and non-wheat flours is that non-wheat flours contain either less gluten or no gluten at all. Gluten is a type of protein that provides structure to dough, gives bread its chewiness, and contributes to the pleasing texture of other baked goods.

There are many types of wheat. Hard wheat is high in protein and gluten; flour ground from hard wheat is the best choice for kneaded breads. Soft wheat and spelt are types of wheat that have less protein and gluten and are therefore excellent for making quick breads. The best-known soft-wheat flour is whole-wheat pastry flour (make sure the label says "pastry"), more often found in health-food stores than in supermarkets.

Recently available and increasingly popular, white whole-wheat flour is made from hard, white wheat. Because the bran layer has relatively few tanins, the flour is lighter in color and sweeter in taste than flour ground from other wheat varieties. When milled very fine, white whole-wheat flour produces delightful quick breads. It's available in some supermarkets and health-food stores, and by mail order from King Arthur Flour.

Grains such as rye and barley have less gluten than wheat. Therefore these flours and gluten-free flours—those ground from gluten-free grains—must be combined with wheat or another proteinlike ingredient to give baked products good structure. (Anyone interested in learning more about this complicated subject will find Harold McGee's *On Food and Cooking* very informative.)

A growing number of people are being diagnosed with celiac disease, meaning that their bodies cannot digest gluten. As a result, we now have easy access to many whole-grain flours that are gluten-free. Some of these flours—like quinoa and amaranth—are fine sources of protein and can be used to replace up to 25 percent of the wheat flour in baked goods, but be prepared for variations in taste and texture.

For more information on whole-grain flours and related subjects, a fine reference is *New Good Food: Essential Ingredients for Cooking and Eating Well* by Margaret M. Wittenberg.

Baking with Whole-Grain Flours

Since this is a book for busy cooks, I have not included recipes for whole-grain yeast breads—a subject that has been covered in depth by others. Instead I've focused on quick breads—baked goods that rise with the help of baking powder, baking soda, and heat in a matter of minutes. In this category I've created homemade whole-grain mixes for pancakes, biscuits, muffins, savory mini-loaves, cakes, cookies, and pie crusts so that you can make these treats quickly and easily on a whim.

I am constantly surprised to see quick-bread recipes using half whole-grain flour and half all-purpose since I have had wonderful results using all whole-grain flours. Here are a few general rules that I follow when developing recipes. Use them to create whole-grain versions of some of your favorite baked goods.

- Substitute whole-wheat pastry flour, white whole-wheat flour, or spelt flour for the all-purpose flour in a standard recipe. Choose whole-wheat pastry flour when you want a very light crumb, spelt flour for a slightly sturdier product.
- Use a combination of baking powder (1 teaspoon per cup of flour) and baking soda (¼ to ½ teaspoon per recipe) for a good rise. (Baking soda also promotes browning.)
- Always include an acidic ingredient like buttermilk or yogurt to maximize the action of the baking soda.
- To achieve even baking and avoid soggy centers, use mini–loaf pans, muffin cups, or shallow cake pans rather than larger pans.
- Add chopped nuts or minced dried fruit to distract from the slightly coarser texture of whole-grain baked goods.
- Since the bran absorbs liquid, sometimes the batter will require slightly more liquid than called for in a standard recipe.
- Don't tell anyone that the goodies are baked with whole-grain flour until after you've received some compliments.

Whole-Grain Flours at a Glance

TYPE	EASY TO GRIND AT HOME?	TASTE	TEXTURE IN BAKED GOODS
Amaranth (GF)	No	Cornlike	Moist, heavy
Barley	Yes, from flakes	Mild, slightly sweet	Moist, silky
Buckwheat (GF)	Yes, from whole groats	Earthy	Heavy
Cornmeal, yellow (GF)	No	Strong corn taste	Grainy, dry, heavy
Millet (GF)	No	Can be bitter, best to avoid	Dry
Oat (GF, but can be risky for celiacs)	Yes, from flakes	Sweet	Moist, silky
Quinoa (GF)	Yes, from flakes	Distinctly vegetal	Light
Rice, brown (GF)	No	Sweet, nutty	Dry, sandy
Rye	Yes, from flakes	Mild	Moist
Spelt (a cousin of wheat)	Yes, from flakes	Mild, slightly nutty	Pleasing
White whole wheat	No	Slightly sweet	Pleasing
Whole-wheat pastry	No	Slightly sweet	Light

GF = GLUTEN-FREE

stand-alone
soups

Chicken, Barley, and Vegetable Soup

Barley Soup with Lamb and Chickpeas

Farro Minestrone

Millet Vegetable Soup

Basil-Scented Oat and Tomato Soup

Squash Bisque with Curried Popcorn

Italian Vegetable Soup with Quinoa

10-Minute Quinoa Soup with Avocado and Corn

Cabbage Soup with Brown Rice, Cannellini, and Gremolata

Curried Black Rice–Lentil Soup with Spinach

Gingered Carrot Soup with Wild Rice and Cranberries

Soba Noodle Soup with Asian Vegetables and Shrimp

chicken, barley, and vegetable soup

Like rolled oats, barley flakes cook very quickly, creating the kind of hearty comfort that's so appealing in a homespun soup. Adding barley also ups the nutritional ante from traditional chicken and rice soup or chicken noodle. The flakes added at the start will come close to dissolving, giving the soup body, while those added toward the end will retain their shape and texture.

SERVES 4

---

1 tablespoon unsalted butter or olive oil

¼ teaspoon dried thyme

⅛ teaspoon granulated garlic

1 quart low-sodium chicken broth

½ cup (½ ounce) loosely packed dried
   mushrooms, snipped into bits and quickly
   rinsed

1 pound skinless, boneless chicken thighs or
   breasts

1 can (15 ounces) navy or Great Northern
   beans, drained and rinsed

1½ cups coarsely grated carrots

1¼ cups barley flakes

1 cup frozen peas

¼ cup chopped fresh dill

Salt and freshly ground black pepper

1 to 2 tablespoons freshly squeezed lemon juice
   (optional)

SPEED TIP: Rehydrate the dried mushrooms right in the soup instead of soaking them in advance.

In a heavy 6-quart soup pot, melt the butter over medium heat. Stir in the thyme and garlic, and cook for 30 seconds. Add the broth, 2 cups of water, the mushrooms, chicken, beans, carrots, and ½ cup of the barley flakes. Bring to a boil over high heat.

Reduce the heat to medium low. Cover and simmer until the chicken is no longer pink in the center, 7 to 15 minutes, depending upon size.

Transfer the chicken to a cutting board. Stir the remaining ¾ cup of barley into the soup, and continue to simmer, uncovered, until the barley is tender, about 8 minutes.

When the chicken is cool enough to handle, shred or dice the meat. Return it to the pot along with the peas and dill. Add salt and pepper to taste and bring to a simmer. Once the peas are defrosted and the chicken is warm, turn off the heat. Before serving, stir in a little lemon juice, if desired, to sharpen the flavors.

OTHER IDEAS

• Use quick-cooking barley or rolled oats instead of barley flakes.

• Use frozen, cut string beans instead of peas. Add them after removing the cooked chicken.

• Substitute cannellini beans for the navy beans.

barley soup with lamb and chickpeas

Lamb is often paired with bulgur, but I find that barley produces a heartier soup and marries equally well with the mint and chickpeas that are common in Middle Eastern cooking. Floating a few lemon slices on top of this soup adds a nice finishing touch.

SERVES 6

1 pound ground lamb

1 cup diced red onion

1 teaspoon ground cumin

½ teaspoon crushed red pepper flakes

Scant ¼ teaspoon ground cinnamon

1 tablespoon olive oil (optional)

1 cup quick-cooking barley

1 can (28 ounces) diced tomatoes, with liquid

1 can (15 ounces) chickpeas, drained and rinsed

1 quart low-sodium chicken or vegetable broth

2 to 3 teaspoons dried mint leaves (you can open a few peppermint tea bags), to taste

Salt and freshly ground black pepper

Freshly squeezed lemon juice (optional)

8 very thin slices of lemon, seeded and quartered

SPEED TIP: Ground lamb cooks much more quickly than cubed and still adds terrific flavor.

Place the lamb in a heavy 6-quart soup pot and set over high heat. When the lamb begins to release fat, stir in the onion, cumin, red pepper flakes, and cinnamon. Add a little olive oil if the lamb doesn't release enough fat to prevent sticking. After 2 minutes, stir in the barley and continue cooking over medium-high heat for 1 minute.

Stir in the diced tomatoes (with liquid), chickpeas, broth, and 3 cups of water. Add the mint leaves, and salt and pepper to taste.

Bring to a boil over high heat. Cover and boil over medium heat until the barley is tender, about 10 minutes. Stir occasionally to prevent the grains from settling to the bottom. Add another cup of water during this time if the soup becomes too thick.

Before serving, add lemon juice, if needed, to sharpen the flavors.

Ladle into large bowls and float a few lemon slices on top.

OTHER IDEAS

• Omit the dried mint and stir in ¼ cup chopped fresh mint at the end.

• Add chopped fresh cilantro just before serving.

• Stir in harissa to taste.

• Omit the water to make a stew rather than a soup.

farro minestrone

Farro, an ancient cousin of the wheat berry, is a toothsome and lovable grain. It cooks quickly and always remains pleasantly chewy. Most farro available here is imported from Italy, so the grain feels right at home in a minestrone.

SERVES 4

2 tablespoons olive oil

1 medium onion, coarsely chopped

2 teaspoons dried Italian seasoning blend

½ teaspoon granulated garlic

1 quart low-sodium chicken or vegetable broth

1 cup semi-pearled farro

1 can (28 ounces) peeled tomatoes, preferably fire-roasted, with liquid

1 can (15 ounces) cannellini beans, drained and rinsed

1 medium zucchini, quartered lengthwise and cut into ½-inch slices

3 tablespoons chopped fresh parsley

¼ cup grated Romano cheese, plus more to pass at the table

Salt and freshly ground black pepper

2 to 3 teaspoons balsamic vinegar (optional)

Pinch of sugar (optional)

SPEED TIP: Use semi-pearled farro—the kind most commonly imported from Italy—which cooks in about half the time of farro with all of its bran intact.

In a heavy 6-quart soup pot, heat 1 tablespoon of the oil over medium-high heat. Stir in the onion and cook until lightly browned, about 3 minutes. Stir in the Italian seasoning and garlic and cook for 20 seconds.

Stir in the broth and the farro. Bring to a boil over high heat. Cover, reduce the heat slightly, and cook for 10 minutes.

Add the tomatoes and squash them against the side of the pot with a large spoon. Stir in the cannellini and zucchini. Cover and cook over medium heat until the farro and zucchini are tender, 10 to 15 minutes longer.

Stir in the parsley, cheese, remaining tablespoon of oil, and salt and pepper to taste. If needed, balance the flavors with a bit of balsamic and sugar.

OTHER IDEAS

• Shortly before serving, stir in 1 bunch chopped arugula or a 6-ounce bag baby spinach.

• Substitute quick-cooking barley for the farro. Cook for only 2 minutes before adding the tomatoes.

• Use chickpeas instead of cannellini.

• Instead of or in addition to the zucchini, add a 10-ounce package frozen string beans or 1 cup frozen peas.

millet vegetable soup

Here is a thick and comforting soup that goes down easy, warming you on a cold, winter's day. A decorative drizzle of buttermilk at the finish gives it a touch of elegance.

Millet is a thirsty grain that becomes soft and mellow when cooked in ample liquid. Using buttermilk as part of the liquid adds creaminess and a little tang. The soup thickens on standing; enjoy it that way or have extra broth at the ready for thinning it.

Serve the soup with something crisp and crunchy like a mixed salad or steamed vegetable. And perhaps a Savory Mini-Loaf (page 169).

SERVES 4

---

1 cup millet grits or 1 cup whole millet

2 tablespoons (¼ stick) unsalted butter or
   olive oil

1 cup chopped leeks (white and light green
   parts) or onion

1 teaspoon dried tarragon

1½ quarts low-sodium chicken or vegetable
   broth

1 package (10 ounces) mixed frozen carrots,
   corn, and peas (sometimes called classic mix)

1 to 1½ cups well-shaken buttermilk, plus a bit
   more for serving

Salt and freshly ground black pepper

SPEED TIP: Using millet grits instead of whole millet cuts the cooking time in half.

If using whole millet, grind it to grits in three or four batches in a spice grinder. It's okay if the grits vary in size.

Set a heavy 6-quart soup pot over medium heat. Add the millet and toast, stirring frequently, until the millet emits a distinct cornlike aroma, about 3 minutes. Transfer the millet to a bowl.

Add the butter to the soup pot, and as it melts, stir in the leeks. Cook until the leeks begin to wilt, about 4 minutes. Stir in the tarragon and cook for another minute.

Add the broth and millet and bring the soup to a boil over high heat, stirring constantly to prevent the grains from sinking to the bottom. If lumps develop, squash them against the side of the pot. Cover and simmer over medium-low heat, stirring frequently, until the millet is just about tender, 10 to 12 minutes.

Stir in the frozen vegetables. Cover and continue cooking until the vegetables and millet are tender, 3 to 5 minutes. Stir in enough buttermilk to give the broth the creaminess of a pureed split-pea soup. Season well with salt and pepper.

Ladle into bowls. Drizzle a little buttermilk in a swirl on the top of each portion.

OTHER IDEAS
- Use herbes de Provence instead of tarragon.
- Substitute frozen asparagus tips or petite peas for the classic mix.
- Add 1 more cup of broth and omit the buttermilk.

basil-scented oat and tomato soup

The last-minute addition of store-bought pesto and a little fresh lemon zest transforms this simple soup into something special. But the real cook's secret is the steel-cut oats, which give the soup satisfying body and a beautiful surface sheen. The oats also make the soup quite filling.

SERVES 4

½ cup steel-cut oats

1 can (28 ounces) diced tomatoes, preferably fire-roasted, with liquid

1 to 2 tablespoons store-bought basil pesto

Salt

Grated zest of 1 small lemon

SPEED TIP: Use store-bought pesto enlivened with fresh lemon zest to add complex flavor and richness fast.

In a heavy 6-quart soup pot bring 4 cups of water and the oats to a boil. Cover and cook over medium heat for 15 minutes, taking care to avoid boil-overs.

Stir in the tomatoes. Cover and continue to cook, stirring occasionally, until the oats are tender, 15 to 20 minutes more. Stir in the pesto and salt to taste.

Ladle into soup bowls. Grate lemon zest on top of each portion before serving.

OTHER IDEAS
• Balance the final flavor with a little sugar or honey and/or a few drops of balsamic vinegar.
• Add ¼ teaspoon crushed red pepper flakes with the tomatoes.
• Swap out 2 cups water for 2 cups vegetable or chicken broth.

In the world of whole grains, there's a thin line between soups and stews. Start off with a soup and within an hour or so, the thirsty grains drink up the broth and the soup becomes a stew.

So please know that the division of recipes between Stand-Alone Soups and Hearty Stews is somewhat artificial. If the recipe starts off with 6 cups or more liquid, it begins life as a soup. With 4 cups or less liquid, it starts off as a stew.

But one thing I can guarantee: any grain soup given an hour on its own recognizance will always turn into a stew. Serve it quickly or keep lots of extra chicken broth at the ready if you are determined to have soup for supper.

squash bisque with curried popcorn

Transform frozen pureed squash into a silken smooth soup by cooking it with oatmeal and broth. It's magic!

For a surprising contrast, garnish each portion with curried popcorn, which makes the soup quite filling and gives it a memorable pop of flavor and crunch.

SERVES 4

For the soup

2 tablespoons unsalted butter

1 tablespoon mild Madras curry powder

¼ teaspoon ground cumin

⅛ teaspoon granulated garlic

Pinch of ground cinnamon

Pinch of cayenne (optional)

1 quart low-sodium chicken or vegetable broth

Salt

⅔ cup oatmeal (old-fashioned rolled oats)

2 packages (12 ounces each) frozen cooked winter squash

¼ cup chopped cilantro

Grated zest of 1 lime (optional)

For the curried popcorn topping

4 cups salted popped popcorn

2 tablespoons (¼ stick) unsalted butter or olive oil

2 teaspoons mild Madras curry powder

½ teaspoon ground cumin

½ teaspoon ground fennel

SPEED TIP: Using frozen pureed squash—a very pure product—obviates the need to peel, cut, and precook fresh squash.

Make the soup: Over medium heat, melt the butter in a heavy 6-quart soup pot. While the butter is melting, stir in the curry powder, cumin, garlic, cinnamon, and cayenne (if using). Toast the spices for 30 seconds.

Add the broth and salt to taste. Stir in the oats. Place the blocks of frozen squash on top. Cover and bring to a boil over high heat. Reduce the heat slightly, cover, and continue cooking until you can break up the squash with a fork, 3 to 5 more minutes. Stir well, cover, and continue cooking over medium heat until the oats are either very soft or partially dissolved, about 5 minutes longer.

While the soup is cooking, prepare the popcorn topping: Place the popcorn in large bowl. Put the butter in a small, heavy-bottomed saucepan and set over medium heat. While the butter is melting, stir in the curry powder, cumin, and fennel. Cook for 1 minute, stirring frequently.

Drizzle the seasoned butter over the popcorn while stirring. Toss and rub the popcorn with your fingers so that it becomes evenly coated with the spiced butter.

When the soup is done, stir in the cilantro and some lime zest, if needed, to sharpen the flavors. Adjust the seasonings. Ladle the soup into bowls and garnish each portion with about ⅓ cup of popcorn. Pass the remaining popcorn at the table.

OTHER IDEAS
• Omit the popcorn and stir the spiced butter into the soup instead. Set a dollop of plain yogurt in the center of each portion. Garnish with chopped fresh cilantro.

italian vegetable soup with quinoa

Quinoa makes a delightful, quick-cooking alternative to rice in this otherwise classic Italian vegetable soup.

SERVES 6

2 to 3 tablespoons olive oil

2 cups coarsely chopped onions

1 teaspoon minced garlic

1 teaspoon dried Italian seasoning blend

1 quart low-sodium vegetable broth

¾ cup quinoa

1 medium carrot, halved lengthwise and cut
   into ¼-inch slices

8 ounces kale

1 can (28 ounces) diced tomatoes, with liquid

1 large zucchini, quartered lengthwise and cut
   into ½-inch chunks

Salt and freshly ground black pepper

¾ cup grated romano cheese

SPEED TIP: Using a store-bought Italian seasoning blend is a fast way to add numerous herbs and spices without measuring them out individually.

Heat 2 tablespoons of oil in a heavy 6-quart soup pot. Stir in the onions and garlic and cook over medium-high heat, stirring frequently, until the onions are lightly browned, about 3 minutes. Stir in the Italian seasoning and cook for another minute.

Add the broth and 4 cups of water and bring to a boil. Stir in the quinoa and carrot, and boil uncovered for 5 minutes.

Meanwhile, strip the kale leaves from the stems and finely chop the leaves. Discard fibrous stems and slice thin, tender stems. Dunk in a large bowl full of water to remove any grit. Drain.

Add the tomatoes, kale, and zucchini. Add salt and pepper to taste. Return to a boil over high heat. Lower the heat to medium and cook, covered, until the vegetables and quinoa are tender, 7 to 8 minutes more. (When tender, the quinoa will have no opaque white dot in the center.)

Stir in ¼ cup of the cheese and a tablespoon of olive oil, if needed, to balance the acidity of the tomatoes. Adjust the seasonings. Ladle the soup into bowls, sprinkling a tablespoon of cheese on top of each portion. Pass the remaining cheese in a bowl at the table.

OTHER IDEAS
• **Instead of kale, use collards, Swiss chard, or broccoli rabe, using all of their stems.**
• **Try a parsnip instead of or in addition to the carrot.**

10-minute quinoa soup with avocado and corn

Here's a soup you can get on the table moments after the urge strikes. Quick-cooking quinoa flakes—quinoa's version of rolled oats—give the soup body and substance, avocado makes it lusciously rich, corn gives it bright crunch, and salsa offers pizzazz. Use a mild or hot salsa, as you prefer.

SERVES 3 TO 4

4 cups chicken or vegetable broth

1 cup quinoa flakes

1 cup frozen corn

¼ to ⅓ cup chunky salsa, to taste

1 ripe but firm Hass avocado, diced

Salt

¼ cup chopped fresh cilantro

Lime wedges, for serving

SPEED TIP: Adding a good store-bought salsa instead of a can of plain, diced tomatoes adds complex flavor by the spoonful.

In a 4-quart soup pot, bring the broth to a rapid boil over high heat. Stir in the quinoa flakes and boil uncovered over medium-high heat for 4 minutes.

Stir in the corn and salsa and continue cooking until the soup is thick and glossy, 1 to 2 minutes.

Turn off the heat and stir in the avocado, salt to taste, and cilantro. Serve in large bowls, accompanied with lime wedges.

OTHER IDEAS
• Add 1 cup drained and rinsed canned black beans with the corn.
• Add 1 or 2 cups of finely chopped cooked chicken or turkey with the salsa.

cabbage soup with brown rice, cannellini, and gremolata

Here is one of those warming Italian farmhouse soups, memorable in its simplicity. To give it some contemporary bling, add a last-minute sprinkle of gremolata, made by mincing fresh rosemary, garlic, and lemon zest together.

SERVES 6

For the soup

2 tablespoons olive oil

1 medium onion, coarsely chopped

5 cloves garlic, coarsely chopped

3 tablespoons tomato paste

1 tablespoon dried Italian seasoning blend

1 teaspoon crushed fennel seeds

½ teaspoon crushed red pepper flakes

3 tablespoons balsamic vinegar, plus more for serving

1 quart low-sodium chicken or vegetable broth

1½ pounds green cabbage, shredded (about 8 cups)

½ cup oil-cured black olives (pitting optional)

1 teaspoon salt

1 cup Minute brown rice

1 can (15 ounces) cannellini beans, drained and rinsed

½ cup grated Pecorino cheese, for serving

For the gremolata

1 large lemon

2 tablespoons fresh rosemary

1 large clove garlic, peeled and thinly sliced

SPEED TIP: Buy preshredded packaged cabbage.

Make the soup: Heat the oil in a heavy 6-quart soup pot over medium-high heat. Add the onion and cook, stirring occasionally, until lightly browned, about 3 minutes. Stir in the garlic and cook for another minute.

Turn the heat down to low. Stir in the tomato paste, Italian seasoning, fennel seeds, and red pepper flakes and cook for 1 minute while stirring. Stir in the balsamic vinegar and cook until it evaporates, taking care to scrape up any browned bits stuck to the bottom or the pot.

Add the broth, 3 cups of water, the cabbage, olives, and salt. Cover, bring to a boil, and cook over medium-high heat for 5 minutes.

Stir in the rice and cannellini. Cover and cook over medium heat until the rice is tender, about 10 minutes.

Meanwhile prepare the gremolata: With a vegetable peeler, using gentle pressure, remove the lemon zest (yellow part only) in thin strips. Place the zest, rosemary, and garlic slices in a small pile on a cutting board and finely chop.

Ladle the soup into bowls. Drizzle about ¼ teaspoon of balsamic vinegar on top of each portion and sprinkle lightly with gremolata. Serve the grated cheese in a bowl at the table.

curried black rice–lentil soup with spinach

Although it cooks in under 40 minutes, the complex flavor of this soup suggests long simmering. Black rice adds exotic beauty and a touch of sweetness.

Just before serving, make the soup explode with flavor by swirling in a few tablespoons of yogurt laced with store-bought Indian eggplant pickle. Patak's Brinjal Pickle is a good choice.

SERVES 6

2 tablespoons peanut or coconut oil

2 tablespoons minced dried onion

1½ teaspoons whole cumin seeds

2 tablespoons mild Madras curry powder

½ teaspoon granulated garlic

6 cups low-sodium chicken or vegetable broth, plus more if needed

1 cup brown lentils

1 cup Thai or Chinese black rice

1 can (15 ounces) diced tomatoes, with liquid

1 package (12 ounces) frozen spinach

Salt

1 cup low-fat plain yogurt

1 to 2 tablespoons prepared eggplant pickle, to taste

SPEED TIP: Combining yogurt with a prepared spicy pickle creates an instant, zesty topping.

In a heavy 6-quart soup pot, heat the oil over medium heat. Stir in the onion and cumin seeds and toast, stirring frequently, until the onion is lightly browned, 1 to 2 minutes. Turn off the heat. Stir in the curry powder and garlic, and let sit in the hot oil for 15 seconds.

Stir in the broth, 2 cups of water, the lentils, and rice. Bring to a boil over high heat. Cover and continue cooking over medium-high heat for 15 minutes.

Add the tomatoes and the block of spinach. Taste, and add more curry powder, if needed. Cover and boil over medium-high heat for 10 minutes. Break up the block of spinach and stir it in. Add salt to taste. If the soup is too thick, stir in additional broth. Continue cooking until the lentils and rice are tender, about 5 minutes longer.

In a small bowl, blend the yogurt and eggplant pickle to taste. Ladle the soup into bowls and drizzle some of the yogurt over each portion. Use a spoon to swirl it around the surface of the soup. Serve extra yogurt topping at the table.

OTHER IDEAS

• Use mango chutney instead of eggplant pickle in the swirl.

• Add 2 tablespoons chopped fresh cilantro to the yogurt and/or 3 tablespoons chopped fresh cilantro to the soup at the end.

gingered carrot soup with wild rice and cranberries

There are lots of interesting textures and flavors in this festive soup. The last-minute addition of dried cranberries and curried popcorn provides plenty of chew and crunch. Buttermilk enriches the soup, giving it tang and a creamy finish. Serve the soup with corn bread and a salad.

SERVES 4

1 pound carrots

1 tablespoon unsalted butter

1 medium onion, finely chopped

2 teaspoons mild Madras curry powder

1 teaspoon fennel seeds, chopped

Salt

5 cups low-sodium chicken or vegetable broth

⅔ cup instant wild rice

1 teaspoon grated fresh ginger

1½ cups well-shaken buttermilk

½ cup dried cranberries

3 tablespoons chopped fresh cilantro

2 cups curried popcorn (see page 41)

SPEED TIP: For faster prep, use a 1-pound bag of baby carrots and pop them right into the processor.

Cut the carrots into large chunks. Coarsely chop them in a food processor. Set aside.

In a heavy 6-quart soup pot, heat the butter over medium-high heat. Add the onion and cook, stirring occasionally, for 2 minutes. Stir in the curry powder and fennel seeds, and cook for an additional minute.

Stir in the carrots and season with salt. Continue cooking for 3 minutes, stirring frequently. Add the broth, cover, and boil for 3 minutes.

Stir in the wild rice, cover, and cook over medium heat for 5 minutes. Stir in the ginger and cook uncovered until the carrots and wild rice are tender, 1 to 3 minutes longer. Add salt to taste.

Meanwhile, pour the buttermilk into a small bowl, ladle ½ cup of the hot broth into the buttermilk, and stir. When the soup is done, stir this mixture into the pot. Add the cranberries plus 2 tablespoons of the cilantro.

Ladle the soup into bowls. Garnish with the remaining tablespoon of cilantro and some curried popcorn. Serve extra popcorn in a bowl at the table.

OTHER IDEAS

• Use Minute brown rice instead of wild rice. Cooking time remains the same.

• Omit the popcorn garnish. Stir 1½ teaspoons additional minced ginger into the soup along with the cilantro. Set a dollop of plain yogurt on top of each portion.

soba noodle soup with asian vegetables and shrimp

Soba is the Japanese name for buckwheat noodles. In this recipe, you can use either 100 percent buckwheat noodles or those that are a blend of buckwheat and whole wheat. If you have trouble finding soba, feel free to substitute whole-wheat or brown rice spaghetti.

This tasty soup requires almost no preparation and cooks in about 15 minutes. It tastes best when freshly made since the noodles continue to absorb water and get very soft if the dish sits.

Since the noodles and frozen vegetables are cooked right in the soup, check the package directions for the minimum cooking times of both before you begin. Subtract the difference; then give the ingredient that requires more cooking an appropriately timed head start.

SERVES 4

2 teaspoons toasted sesame oil, plus more if
 needed
1 bunch scallions, thinly sliced (keep white and
 green parts separate)
3 cups low-sodium chicken or vegetable broth
1 package (12 ounces) Asian frozen vegetables
6 ounces whole-wheat soba
8 to 12 ounces small or medium shrimp, peeled
 and cleaned
1 tablespoon minced fresh ginger

2 teaspoons Japanese soy sauce (tamari or shoyu), or to
 taste
¼ to ½ teaspoon chile-garlic paste or hot-pepper sesame
 oil, to taste

SPEED TIP: Using an Asian-style blend of frozen vegetables—such as one that contains edamame or is labeled "stir-fry"—obviates the need for time-consuming veggie prep.

In a heavy 6-quart soup pot, heat the oil over medium heat. Stir in the sliced scallion whites. Cook for 1 minute. Add the broth and 3 cups of water. Bring to a boil over high heat.

Add either the frozen vegetables or the soba—whichever one takes the longest to cook. Return to a boil. Cook for the number of minutes required for a head start and then add the other ingredient. Cook until the noodles are just short of done.

Stir in the shrimp, ginger, soy sauce, and chile-garlic paste. Cook until the vegetables and noodles are tender and the shrimp turn pink, about 2 minutes. Stir in the scallion greens. Add more sesame oil, if needed.

OTHER IDEAS
• Just before serving, stir in 1 sheet of nori sea vegetable (wrapping for sushi), torn into pieces. Highly recommended.

hearty
stews

Barley Cioppino

Hominy and Kidney Bean Chili

Provençal Salmon Stew with Quinoa

Southwestern Quinoa Stew with Squash, Black Beans, and Corn

Steamed Mussels with Garlicky Brown Rice and White Beans

Andouille, Shrimp, and Brown Rice Gumbo

Portuguese Stew with Brown Rice, Chorizo, and Kale

Thai Fish Curry with Brown Rice

Beef and Noodle Hot Pot

barley cioppino

Adding quick-cooking barley to this elegant, stream-lined version of San Franciscan seafood stew gives it more substance and a very pleasing texture.

SERVES 4

1 tablespoon olive oil

1 medium onion, coarsely chopped

2 teaspoons minced garlic

1 teaspoon dried Italian seasoning blend

½ cup dry white wine or dry vermouth

1 can (15 ounces) diced tomatoes, with liquid

1 cup quick-cooking barley

1 pound mussels, rinsed and debearded

12 ounces medium shrimp, peeled and cleaned

8 ounces sea scallops, halved if large

Grated zest of 1 large lemon

2 tablespoons chopped fresh parsley, plus more for serving

Salt and freshly ground black pepper

In a heavy 12-inch sauté pan or high-sided skillet, heat the oil over medium-high heat. Add the onion and cook for 2 minutes, stirring frequently. Stir in the garlic and Italian seasoning, and continue cooking and stirring for 1 more minute.

Add the wine and cook until most of it evaporates, 1 to 2 minutes. Stir in the tomatoes and 2 cups of water and bring to a boil. Add the barley, cover, and cook over medium heat for 5 minutes.

Scatter the mussels over the barley, cover, and cook over medium-high heat until the mussels open wide, 3 to 4 minutes.

Lift the mussels with tongs or a slotted spoon and divide them among four large, shallow soup bowls. (It's fine if some barley is scattered here and there.) Discard any mussels that have not opened.

Stir the shrimp, scallops, lemon zest, and parsley into the barley. Season with salt and pepper to taste. Cook uncovered over medium-high heat, stirring frequently, until the seafood is opaque, 1 to 3 minutes. Spoon the stew over the mussels and garnish with a light sprinkling of parsley.

OTHER IDEAS

• Omit the mussels and increase the quantity of shrimp and scallops to 1 pound each. Omit the water and substitute 1 bottle (13 fluid ounces) clam juice; increase the canned tomatoes to 28 ounces. Cook the barley for 9 minutes before adding the shrimp and scallops.

• Add ½ teaspoon crushed red pepper flakes with the Italian seasoning.

hominy and kidney bean chili

It takes a few hours to cook dried hominy from scratch, but ready-to-eat chewy nuggets of this large-kernel field corn are readily available in cans, usually in the Latin section of supermarkets.

Combine the hominy with mahogany kidney beans to make a hearty, protein-rich, vegetarian stew. Diced tomatoes brighten the mix, and chunks of zucchini cooked tender-crisp make a good counterpart to the mellow beans and hominy. Serve the chili with Southwestern Mini-Loaves (page 169), if you like.

SERVES 4 TO 6

1 tablespoon olive oil

1 medium onion, coarsely chopped

2 teaspoons chili powder, plus more to taste

½ teaspoon ground cumin

½ teaspoon granulated garlic

⅛ teaspoon ground cinnamon

1 teaspoon dried oregano

2 cans (14.5 ounces each) diced tomatoes with green chiles, preferably fire-roasted, with liquid

1 can (15 ounces) white or yellow hominy, drained and rinsed

1 can (15 ounces) red kidney beans, drained and rinsed

2 medium zucchini, cut into 1-inch chunks

Salt and freshly ground black pepper

1 cup diced roasted red bell pepper, preferably fire-roasted

¼ cup chopped fresh cilantro, plus more for serving

Lime wedges, for serving

½ cup shredded sharp Cheddar cheese, for serving

> **SPEED TIP:** Using canned diced tomatoes with chiles included saves you the trouble of buying and preparing fresh chilies.

In a heavy 4-quart Dutch oven, heat the oil. Stir in the onion and cook over medium-high heat, stirring frequently, until it begins to soften, 2 to 3 minutes. Lower the heat to medium. Stir in the chili powder, cumin, garlic, and cinnamon, and cook for another minute. Stir in the oregano.

Add the tomatoes, hominy, beans, and zucchini. Season to taste with salt and pepper, and additional chili powder, if needed. Bring to a boil.

Cover, reduce the heat, and simmer until the zucchini is tender but still firm, 8 to 12 minutes.

Stir in the roasted red pepper and cilantro just before serving. Ladle into soup bowls and accompany with bowls of lime wedges and grated cheese.

OTHER IDEAS

• If you are not partial to spicy food, use diced tomatoes without added chiles.

• If you like very hot food, add pureed chipotle in adobo to taste along with the chili powder.

• Brown ½ to 1 pound of ground pork in the heated oil. Then stir in the onion and proceed as directed.

provençal salmon stew with quinoa

Because it is so versatile and quick-cooking, I often think of quinoa when I want to include a grain in a one-pot dinner. Here you'll find it paired with salmon in a stew that is flavored with ingredients common to the Provençal kitchen.

SERVES 4

1 tablespoon olive oil

1 cup diced onion

¾ teaspoon dried thyme

½ teaspoon minced garlic

½ teaspoon anchovy paste

½ cup dry white wine or vermouth

2 bottles (13 ounces each) clam juice

1 cup quinoa

1 can (15 ounces) diced tomatoes, with liquid

¼ cup Niçoise or other small black olives
   (pitting optional)

¼ teaspoon salt, plus more to taste

1 pound skinless salmon fillets, cut into 1-inch
   chunks

3 tablespoons chopped fresh parsley, plus more
   for garnish

Grated zest of 1 large lemon

1 to 2 tablespoons freshly squeezed lemon
   juice, to taste

> **SPEED TIP:** Just the tiniest bit of anchovy paste creates complexity and pulls together the various flavors in a dish. Few people will realize it's there.

In a heavy 12-inch sauté pan or large skillet, heat the oil over medium-high heat. Add the onion, thyme, and garlic, and cook, stirring frequently, until the onion is lightly browned, 3 to 4 minutes. Stir in the anchovy paste and cook for 30 seconds more.

Stir in the wine and cook until it evaporates, about 2 minutes. Add the clam juice and bring to a boil. Stir in the quinoa, cover, and cook over medium heat for 8 minutes. Stir in the tomatoes, olives, and salt. Return to a boil. Cover and continue cooking until the quinoa is almost done, about 5 minutes longer. (If the quinoa has a substantial white dot of starch in the center, continue cooking until the dot is tiny.)

Add a little water if the mixture is no longer loose and soupy. Gently stir in the salmon. Cover and cook over medium heat until the salmon is cooked through to the center and the quinoa is tender, 2 to 3 minutes. Gently stir in the parsley, lemon zest and juice, plus additional salt, if needed.

Serve in large, shallow bowls, garnished with additional parsley.

OTHER IDEAS
• Substitute 1 pound peeled, medium shrimp for the salmon. Cook uncovered.

southwestern quinoa stew with squash, black beans, and corn

Quinoa is grown in the highland Andes, so it's a natural to combine this high-protein grain with other ingredients indigenous to the Americas. Pureed winter squash thickens the stew, offering bright color at the same time.

SERVES 4 TO 6

1 tablespoon olive oil

2 teaspoons minced dried onion

½ teaspoon dried oregano

¼ teaspoon granulated garlic

1 quart low-sodium chicken or vegetable broth

1 cup quinoa

1 teaspoon chipotle in adobo, mashed

1 package (10 ounces) frozen cooked winter squash

1 can (15 ounces) black beans, drained and rinsed

1 cup frozen corn

⅓ cup diced fire-roasted red bell pepper

¼ cup chopped fresh cilantro

Salt

In a heavy 3-quart Dutch oven, heat the oil over medium-high heat. Stir in the onion, oregano, and garlic, and cook for 10 seconds.

Add the broth and 2 cups of water. Bring to a boil over high heat. Add the quinoa and boil uncovered over medium-high heat for 10 minutes.

Stir in the chipotle in adobo, and add the block of squash. Turn the heat to high, cover, and continue cooking until you can break up the squash and stir it into the stew, 3 to 4 minutes.

Stir in the beans. Reduce the heat to medium. Continue cooking until there is no solid white dot of starch at the center of the quinoa, 1 to 3 minutes longer. Stir in the corn, roasted red pepper, cilantro, and salt to taste. Cook uncovered, just until the corn is defrosted, another minute or so.

Ladle into soup bowls.

OTHERS IDEAS
• **Stir a diced, ripe avocado into the stew just before serving.**
• **Add chopped cooked turkey or fully cooked turkey sausage along with the corn.**
• **Garnish each portion with popcorn.**

steamed mussels with garlicky brown rice and white beans

When mussels steam open, they release a most exquisite broth, creating an irresistibly briny background for soft, chewy rice and mellow beans. The rice absorbs the mussel broth, making it especially delicious.

The recipe can easily be doubled, but to facilitate even cooking, use a pan wide enough to avoid stacking the mussels in more than two layers.

SERVES 2

1 tablespoon olive oil

¼ cup minced shallots or onion

2 teaspoons minced garlic

½ teaspoon dried oregano

2 tablespoons tomato paste

½ cup dry white wine

1 cup Minute brown rice

2 pounds mussels, rinsed and debearded

1 cup canned cannellini or navy beans

2 tablespoons chopped fresh parsley

Grated zest of 1 lemon

Salt

In a heavy 12-inch sauté pan or high-sided skillet, heat the oil over medium-high heat. Add the shallots and cook for 2 minutes, stirring frequently. Stir in the garlic and oregano and cook for 10 seconds. Stir in the tomato paste and cook another minute.

Stir in the wine and cook until most of it has evaporated, about 2 minutes. Add 2½ cups of water. Bring to a boil. Stir in the rice and ½ teaspoon salt. Cover and cook over medium heat for 2 minutes.

Distribute the mussels on top of the rice. Cover and cook over high heat, shaking the pan occasionally, until the mussels have steamed open, about 5 minutes.

Use a slotted spoon to divide the mussels among two large, shallow soup bowls. (No problem that there will be some rice clinging to the mussels.) Discard any mussels that do not open.

Turn the heat down to medium. Stir in the beans. Cover and cook for 1 minute. If the rice is not tender, cover and let sit off the heat for another minute or two.

Stir the parsley and lemon zest into the rice, and add salt to taste. Ladle the rice, beans, and broth over and around the mussels.

andouille, shrimp, and brown rice gumbo

Bring the flavors of New Orleans to your table with this colorful, filling stew. Although white rice is the grain of choice in traditional Creole cooking, brown rice stands up even better to the assertive flavors of the gumbo.

If you don't consider yourself a fan of okra, try it in this dish, where its taste and texture are in an optimal context. Gumbo is, after all, the African word for okra. I prefer whole okra in this stew, both for looks and texture, but use sliced okra if you prefer bite-sized pieces.

SERVES 3 TO 4

2 packages (12 ounces each) frozen whole okra

2 cups Minute brown rice

2 fully cooked andouille sausages, sliced

1 tablespoon minced dried onion

1½ teaspoons Cajun seasoning blend, plus more
    to taste

½ teaspoon granulated garlic

1 bottle (8 ounces) clam juice

1 can (14.5 ounces) crushed tomatoes

Salt and freshly ground black pepper

1 pound medium shrimp, peeled and cleaned

Tabasco sauce, for serving

SPEED TIP: Using a good-quality spice blend, in this case a zesty Creole blend, adds lots of flavor by the teaspoon.

Place the okra in a large colander and run hot water over them until you can pry apart any that are stuck together. Set aside.

Set a heavy 12-inch sauté pan or high-sided skillet over medium-high heat. Add the rice and toast until aromatic, 3 to 4 minutes, stirring occasionally. Tip the rice into a bowl.

In the same pan, cook the sausages over medium-high heat until lightly browned, 2 to 3 minutes. Stir in the onion, Cajun seasoning, and garlic, and cook for another 30 seconds.

Gradually add the clam juice, tomatoes, and 1 cup of water. Stir in ½ teaspoon salt and a few twists of black pepper. Bring to a boil over high heat.

Stir in the rice, okra, and additional Cajun seasoning, and more salt and pepper, if desired. Cover and cook over medium heat for 7 minutes.

Stir in the shrimp, cover, and cook over medium heat until the shrimp are opaque, and the rice is tender, 2 to 3 minutes.

Ladle into large, shallow bowls. Serve accompanied by a bottle of Tabasco sauce.

OTHER IDEAS
- **Use frozen green beans instead of the okra.**
- **Use diced smoked ham instead of sausage. Skip the browning step.**
- **Add 1 chopped green bell pepper and/or ½ cup diced celery after browning the sausages. Add a little oil, if needed, and cook for 2 minutes before adding the dried onion.**

portuguese stew with brown rice, chorizo, and kale

My inspiration for this dish is the hearty Portuguese caldo verde, a soup of kale and potatoes. Using brown rice instead of potatoes adds a nice chewiness to the mix.

Make sure to use low-sodium broth since the chorizo, which adds a lot of flavor, can be quite salty.

SERVES 5 TO 6

1 bunch kale (12 ounces to 1 pound)

1½ cups Minute brown rice

2 teaspoons minced dried onion

2 cups low-sodium chicken broth

1 can (14.5 ounces) diced tomatoes, with liquid

2 large bay leaves

6 ounces dry-cured chorizo, quartered lengthwise and thinly sliced

1 can (15 ounces) kidney beans, drained and rinsed

Salt and freshly ground black pepper

SPEED TIP: To eliminate veggie prep, buy a 1-pound bag of washed, chopped kale.

Holding the kale in a bunch, slice off and discard the thick, fibrous portion of stem. Slice the remaining stems as thinly as you can. Cut the leaves into ½-inch strips. Wash thoroughly in a large bowl, and drain.

Set a heavy 6-quart (or larger) soup pot over medium-high heat. Add the rice and toast until aromatic, 2 to 3 minutes, stirring occasionally. Stir in the onion and toast for 20 seconds.

Gradually add the broth and 3 cups of water. Stir in the tomatoes, bay leaves, chorizo, and the beans. Cover and bring to a boil over high heat. Uncover and press as much kale as you can into the liquid. Cover and cook until the kale wilts, 1 to 2 minutes. Stir well and add the remaining kale. Cover and continue cooking over high heat until the remaining kale wilts.

Turn the heat down to medium. Stir well. Add salt, if needed, and pepper to taste. Cook uncovered, stirring occasionally, until the kale is tender, the rice is cooked, and the flavors mingle, 5 to 10 minutes longer.

Remove the bay leaves. Adjust the seasonings. Serve in large soup bowls.

OTHER IDEAS
• Use chickpeas instead of kidney beans.
• Add 1 to 2 teaspoons of smoked Spanish paprika when you stir in the dried onion.
• Use 8 ounces fresh chorizo instead of dried. Tip the toasted rice out of the pot, and brown the chorizo in the same pot, and then proceed with the recipe, returning the rice to the pot when the liquid comes to a boil.

thai fish curry with brown rice

Coconut milk is so full of flavor that it can be transformed into the sauce for a memorable curry with the addition of just a few well-chosen seasonings—in this case, Thai curry paste, fish sauce, and fresh cilantro. Spoon the sauce over a mound of freshly cooked brown rice.

SERVES 4

For the rice

2 cups Minute brown rice

½ teaspoon salt

For the fish curry

1 can (13.5 ounces) coconut milk

2 to 3 teaspoons Thai fish sauce

1 teaspoon green or yellow Thai curry paste, plus more to taste

½ teaspoon sugar

1 cup frozen corn kernels

1 can (8 ounces) sliced water chestnuts, drained

1½ to 2 pounds skinless firm white fish fillets, such as cod, scrod, haddock, or halibut, cut into 1½-inch chunks

⅓ cup chopped fresh cilantro

Grated zest of 1 lime

1 tablespoon freshly squeezed lime juice (optional)

SPEED TIP: Make double the amount of rice and use extra to make Any Grain with Sausage and Peppers (page 62) or Chinese Fried Grains and Vegetables with Honey-Mustard Sauce (page 64).

Make the rice: Set a heavy 3-quart pot over medium heat. Add the rice and toast, stirring occasionally, until aromatic, 3 to 4 minutes.

Gradually pour in 1⅓ cups of water and the salt. Cover and reduce the heat so that the water simmers. Cook for 5 minutes. Stir well. Turn off the heat and let steep for 5 minutes.

While the rice is cooking, prepare the curry: In a heavy 12-inch sauté pan or high-sided skillet, blend the coconut milk, ½ cup water, the fish sauce, curry paste, and sugar. Bring to a boil. Stir in the water chestnuts and corn.

Add the fish, cover, and cook over medium heat, stirring occasionally, until the fish turns opaque, 2 to 3 minutes. Stir in ¼ cup of the cilantro and the lime zest. Add lime juice, if needed, to sharpen the flavors.

Spoon the rice into shallow soup bowls. Ladle the fish curry over and around the rice. Garnish with the remaining cilantro.

OTHER IDEAS

• **Reduce the fish to 1 pound and include 8 ounces peeled, medium shrimp. Add the shrimp along with the fish chunks.**
• **Instead of fish sauce, substitute a few drops of Worcestershire sauce and salt to taste.**
• **Use fresh basil instead of cilantro.**

beef and noodle hot pot

With a bow to the flavors of Korea—where garlic is as beloved as beef—this hearty meal-in-a-bowl features soba noodles, made partially or entirely of buckwheat.

This recipe was tested with soba noodles that took 6 minutes to cook. Make adjustments as needed if your package instructions indicate a different timing.

SERVES 4

2 tablespoons peanut or safflower oil

12 ounces boneless beef chuck top steak, trimmed and thinly sliced on the diagonal

4 scallions, thinly sliced (keep white and green parts separate)

2 teaspoons brown sugar

1 pound Chinese or Napa cabbage, coarsely chopped (6 cups)

1 quart low-sodium beef broth

½ teaspoon chile-garlic paste

½ teaspoon granulated garlic, plus more to taste

2 to 3 tablespoons Japanese soy sauce (tamari or shoyu), to taste

8 ounces soba noodles

6 to 8 ounces firm tofu, cubed

8 ounces snow peas, trimmed and sliced into thirds on the diagonal

1 tablespoon finely chopped fresh ginger

1 to 2 teaspoons toasted sesame oil, to taste

OTHER IDEAS

• When you add the snow peas, crack 1 egg per person onto different quadrants of the soup. Cover the pot and simmer until the egg is poached to desired consistency, 2 to 3 minutes. This is great!

• Substitute udon noodles for the soba. Adjust the timing according to package directions.

• For a vegetarian version, omit the beef and use vegetable broth. Increase the tofu to 12 ounces. Poach the eggs as directed above.

• Instead of snow peas, use an 8-ounce package defrosted frozen sugar snap peas or 2 cups defrosted frozen shelled edamame.

SPEED TIP: Beef is easiest to slice when it's partially frozen. Alternatively, purchase thin-sliced beef for stir-fry.

Heat the oil in a heavy 12-inch sauté pan or high-sided skillet. Add the meat and scallion whites. Cook over high heat, stirring occasionally, until the meat loses most of its red color, about 2 minutes. Stir in the brown sugar and cook for another minute.

Stir in the cabbage, cover, and cook until it wilts, about 2 minutes.

Stir in the beef broth, 6 cups of water, chile-garlic paste, garlic, and soy sauce. Cover and bring to a boil over high heat.

Add the noodles, pressing them under the liquid with a large spoon. Stir in the tofu. Cover and cook for 3 minutes. Stir in the scallion greens and snow peas. Continue cooking uncovered until the noodles are tender, 2 to 3 more minutes. Stir in the ginger and adjust the seasonings.

Ladle into large bowls. Drizzle a few drops of sesame oil on top of each portion. Serve immediately. The noodles will continue to soften and absorb broth as the soup sits.

skillet
suppers

Any Grain with Sausage and Peppers

Bulgur with Lamb, Chickpeas, Spinach, and Prunes

Chinese Fried Grains and Vegetables with Honey-Mustard Sauce

Barley Frittata

Morrocan-Spiced Beef Burgers with Harissa Couscous

Ham-and-Egg Couscous "Cake"

Beef Stir-Fry with Soy-Spiked Couscous

Tex-Mex Hominy and Eggs

Quinoa and Mushroom Skillet Pie

Oat-Crusted Turkey Cutlets with Gingered Cranberry Relish

Quinoa-Crusted Chicken Cutlets with Cilantro Pesto

Popcorn-Crusted Turkey Cutlets with Cherry Tomato Salsa

Michael's Quick Brown Rice with Tuna and Green Beans

Soft Chicken Tacos with Smoked Paprika Sour Cream

any grain with sausage and peppers

This recipe offers an Italian and an Asian approach to cooking a fast skillet supper with any cooked grains that you have on hand—or you can quickly whip up a batch of Minute rice or quick-cooking barley while you're doing the chopping.

SERVES 2 TO 3

Italian

2 tablespoons olive oil

1 large onion, halved and thinly sliced

2 teaspoons minced garlic

1 or 2 fully cooked Italian-style sausages, quartered lengthwise and diced

1 large green bell pepper, seeded and cut into thin strips

1 large red bell pepper, seeded and cut into thin strips

2 cups cooked grains

1 to 2 tablespoons store-bought pesto or olive tapenade, to taste

Grated zest of 1 lemon

1 to 2 teaspoons balsamic vinegar, to taste

Chopped fresh basil or parsley (optional)

Salt and freshly ground black pepper

Asian

2 tablespoons peanut or safflower oil

3 scallions, thinly sliced

1 tablespoon chopped fresh ginger

1 teaspoon chopped garlic

1 or 2 fully cooked sausages, quartered lengthwise and diced (choose sausages seasoned with soy sauce or with flavors compatible with the dish)

1 large green bell pepper, seeded and cut into thin strips

1 large red bell pepper, seeded and cut into thin strips

2 cups cooked grains

2 to 3 tablespoons store-bought Thai peanut sauce, to taste

Chopped fresh cilantro (optional)

¼ cup chopped roasted peanuts

Japanese soy sauce (tamari or shoyu), to taste

Heat the oil in a heavy 12-inch skillet over medium-high heat. Add the ingredients that are listed up to and including the sausages, and cook for 3 minutes while stirring. Add the green and red peppers and ⅓ cup of water. Cover and cook over medium heat until the peppers are tender, 3 to 5 minutes.

Stir in the grains and cook until they are hot, 2 to 3 minutes if they have been refrigerated. Add a little more water if the mixture begins sticking to the bottom of the skillet. Turn off the heat and stir in the remaining ingredients. Adjust the seasonings to taste.

bulgur with lamb, chickpeas, spinach, and prunes

In the Middle East, bulgur and dried fruits are often combined with meat, with memorable results.

Serve this dish hot or at room temperature, accompanied by a salad of arugula dressed with a lemony vinaigrette. These sharp and acidic ingredients balance out the richness of the lamb and the sweetness of the prunes.

SERVES 4 TO 6

½ tablespoon olive oil

1 pound ground lamb

2 tablespoons minced dried onion

1 teaspoon ground cinnamon

2 cups low-sodium chicken broth

¾ teaspoon salt

1 teaspoon harissa or ¼ teaspoon crushed red pepper flakes, plus more to taste

1¼ cups coarse bulgur

1 can (15 or 19 ounces) chickpeas, drained and rinsed

10 large pitted prunes, quartered

1 package (10 ounces) frozen chopped spinach

Freshly ground black pepper

⅓ cup pine nuts, toasted

⅓ cup chopped fresh cilantro

SPEED TIP: Since there are many good, strong flavors in this dish, it's an ideal recipe to use minced dried onion instead of taking the time to peel and chop a fresh onion.

Heat the oil in a heavy 12-inch sauté pan or high-sided skillet over high heat. Add the lamb, onion, and cinnamon and cook, stirring occasionally, until the lamb loses its pink color, about 3 minutes. Drain off the fat.

Gradually add the broth, 1 cup of water, and the salt. Blend in the harissa. Bring to a boil.

Stir in the bulgur, chickpeas, and prunes. Set the block of spinach on top. Cover and cook over high heat for 5 minutes.

Break up the spinach and stir it in. Cover and continue cooking over medium heat for 5 minutes. Stir in a bit more water if the mixture seems dry and the bulgur is not quite tender. Adjust the seasonings, adding black pepper to taste and more harissa, if desired. Turn off the heat and let sit for 5 minutes or until ready to serve.

Stir in the pine nuts and ¼ cup cilantro. Garnish individual portions with the remaining cilantro.

chinese fried grains and vegetables with honey-mustard sauce

I've modeled this recipe on the idea of fried rice, and it's a tasty way to use up leftover cooked grains plus whatever vegetables are screaming for attention in your fridge or freezer. Use the recipe as a template for your own combinations and consider the quantities approximations.

Start by quick-steaming the vegetables. Then add cooked grains and a homemade stir-fry-style sauce for the final few minutes. You can make the dish more substantial by adding some cooked meat.

SERVES 3 TO 4

For the sauce

¼ cup Japanese soy sauce (tamari or shoyu)

3 tablespoons mustard, preferably whole grain

2 tablespoons toasted sesame oil

2 tablespoons honey

1 teaspoon granulated garlic

¼ to ½ teaspoon chile-garlic paste or crushed red pepper flakes (optional), to taste

For the vegetables and grains

4 to 5 cups chopped, raw vegetables, such as broccoli, cauliflower, carrots, Brussels sprouts, cabbage, zucchini, and snow peas

2 cups cooked grains, such as brown rice, barley, or quinoa

1 to 2 cups chopped cooked meat (optional)

1 tablespoon minced fresh ginger

OTHER IDEAS

• Use a 1-pound package frozen mixed vegetables for the stir-fry. Run them under hot water briefly and drain well before adding to the pot.

• Once the vegetables are steamed, tip them out. Heat a little oil in the same pot, add 2 beaten eggs and scramble them. Return the vegetables to the pot, add the grains, and continue as directed.

• Add cubed, firm tofu along with the grains.

• Garnish each portion with toasted sesame seeds.

SPEED TIPS: This recipe makes ¾ cup of honey-mustard sauce, but you won't need all of it. Refrigerate the leftover sauce for up to 1 month and make another version of this recipe even more quickly.

Buy chopped vegetables from the salad bar.

Use a store-bought stir-fry sauce.

Make the sauce: In a small jar, combine the soy sauce, mustard, sesame oil, honey, garlic, and chile-garlic paste (if using). Add 3 tablespoons of water and shake well.

Prepare the vegetables and grains: In a heavy 12-inch skillet, bring ¼ cup of water to a boil over high heat. Add the dense vegetables (such as broccoli, carrots, and Brussels sprouts), cover, and steam until almost tender, about 3 minutes. Add the quick-cooking vegetables (such as zucchini and snow peas), cover, and cook until all of the vegetables are tender but still crisp, about 2 minutes more. Add a few tablespoons more water during this time, if needed. Stir in the grains, meat (if using), and ginger.

Shake the sauce and pour on enough to coat the ingredients lightly, usually ¼ to ⅓ cup. Divide among plates and serve.

barley frittata

This frittata makes a wonderful last-minute supper. Unlike some frittatas that are baked, this one is made in a large skillet on top of the stove and then set under the broiler for a final few minutes of browning.

Eggs are essential to a frittata since they bind together whatever ingredients the cook chooses to add. In this recipe, I've created a particularly hearty version by including quick-cooking barley flakes—barley's equivalent to rolled oats. You don't need an extra pot to prepare the barley since it's cooked right in the skillet along with browned onions and bits of salami. At the last minute, the eggs are poured over everything, creating a kind of pancake.

All you need to complete the meal is a tossed green salad or a steamed vegetable.

SERVES 4

1 cup diced salami (4 ounces)

1 cup chopped onion

2 to 3 teaspoons olive oil, if needed

1 teaspoon dried Italian seasoning blend

¼ teaspoon granulated garlic

¼ teaspoon crushed red pepper flakes

¼ teaspoon salt (optional)

1 cup barley flakes

8 large eggs

⅓ cup grated Romano cheese

Freshly grated black pepper

1 cup diced roasted red bell pepper

3 ounces loosely packed, shredded mozzarella, preferably smoked (1 cup)

OTHER IDEAS
• **Use old-fashioned rolled oats instead of the barley flakes.**
• **Use smoked diced ham instead of salami.**
• **For a vegetarian version, omit the salami; add ½ cup frozen peas along with the roasted red pepper.**
• **Add chopped arugula with the roasted red pepper.**
• **Try Gruyère or Cheddar cheese instead of mozzarella.**

SPEED TIP: Use jarred roasted red bell pepper. Fire-roasted peppers are especially tasty.

Preheat the broiler. Heat a heavy 10- or 12-inch ovenproof skillet over medium-high heat. Add the salami and cook, stirring frequently, until it renders some fat, 1 to 2 minutes.

Stir in the onion and some oil, if needed. Cook until the onion is lightly browned, about 3 minutes. Stir in the Italian seasoning, garlic, and red pepper flakes, and cook for another 30 seconds.

Add 1 cup of water and the salt, if using. (The salami and Romano cheese will add enough salt for most people.) Bring to a boil over high heat, taking care to scrape up any browned bits on the bottom of the pan. Stir in the barley flakes. Cover and reduce the heat to low.

Cook until the barley is tender but still firm, about 5 minutes. Stir in a little more water if the mixture becomes dry before the barley is done.

Beat the eggs. Stir in the Romano cheese and season with black pepper to taste.

When the barley is tender, distribute the roasted red pepper on top. Turn the heat to medium. Pour the eggs evenly over the barley. With a rubber spatula, push the barley around the edges of the pan aside, tilting the pan to allow the uncooked egg to seep to the bottom. Continue doing this until the eggs are no longer runny. (It's okay if they still look wet on the top.)

Sprinkle the mozzarella cheese on top of the eggs. Grate on some black pepper. Set the skillet 4 or 5 inches under the broiler until the cheese is melted, 1 to 3 minutes. Let sit for a minute or two before you slice and serve.

moroccan-spiced beef burgers with harissa couscous

Stirring in a spoonful of spicy harissa and some chopped cilantro instantly brings a simple bowl of bland couscous to life. Coating whole-wheat couscous with a tiny bit of oil before adding water keeps the individual grains separate and ensures that the batch will be light and fluffy—an ideal accompaniment to brightly seasoned burgers.

For years it was difficult to find harissa in the United States. Now it's available everywhere. If you don't want to invest in harissa, use any tomato-based chile sauce to heat up the couscous.

SERVES 3 TO 4

For the burgers

1 large egg

½ teaspoon onion powder

½ teaspoon salt

½ teaspoon freshly ground black pepper

½ teaspoon ground cumin

½ teaspoon crushed red pepper flakes

¼ teaspoon ground cinnamon

1 pound ground beef

1 tablespoon olive oil

For the couscous

1 cup whole-wheat couscous

1 teaspoon salt

½ to 1 teaspoon harissa, to taste, plus more to pass at the table

¼ cup chopped fresh cilantro

SPEED TIP: Forming patties smaller than the traditional size of a burger decreases cooking time.

Make the burgers: In a large bowl, beat the egg. Blend in the onion powder, salt, pepper, cumin, red pepper flakes, and cinnamon. Blend the egg mixture into the meat with your hands. Form 8 small patties, each about 1 inch thick.

Heat the oil over medium-high heat in a 12-inch nonstick skillet that has a cover. Arrange the patties in one layer. Brown on both sides and continue cooking until the centers are cooked to desired doneness, 6 to 10 minutes total. Remove the patties to a platter and tent with foil to keep warm. Leave grease in the skillet.

Prepare the couscous: Stir the couscous into the fat remaining in the skillet. Stir in 1 to 1½ cups boiling water (according to package instructions), the salt, and harissa. Cover and let sit off the heat for 5 minutes. Stir in the cilantro as you fluff up the couscous with a fork.

To serve, make a bed of couscous on each plate and set the patties on top. Serve a small bowl of harissa at the table.

OTHER IDEAS

• Use ground pork, veal, or lamb—or a mixture—instead of beef.

• Make 4 large patties instead of 8 small ones, and increase the cooking time.

• Use fresh mint instead of cilantro.

ham-and-egg couscous "cake"

With its melted Cheddar on top, this "cake"—a stove-top pie, chock-full of couscous, dotted with smoked ham, and bound by egg—is pretty enough to serve on a platter and cut at the table.

It makes a nice, light supper, accompanied by a steamed vegetable or salad.

SERVES 3 TO 4

2 teaspoons olive oil

1 teaspoon minced dried onion

¼ teaspoon granulated garlic

½ teaspoon salt

1 cup whole-wheat couscous

4 large eggs

½ cup milk or water

½ teaspoon dried oregano

Freshly ground black pepper

Tabasco sauce

1 cup diced smoked ham

½ cup shredded sharp Cheddar cheese

In an 8- or 9-inch nonstick skillet, heat the oil over medium-high heat. Stir in the onion and garlic and cook for 30 seconds. Stir in 1 to 1½ cups of water (depending upon brand; see package instructions) and ¼ teaspoon of the salt. Bring to a boil, and stir in the couscous. Turn off the heat. Cover and let sit until the water is absorbed, 5 minutes.

Meanwhile, beat the eggs in a bowl. Blend in the milk, remaining ¼ teaspoon salt, the oregano, pepper, and 5 to 10 drops of Tabasco sauce to taste.

When the couscous is tender, stir in the ham. Turn the heat to medium-high. Wait for about 30 seconds. Push the couscous to one side, and add the egg to the empty side of the skillet. After about 20 seconds, stir until the egg and couscous are thoroughly combined. Smooth off the top with the back of a wooden spoon.

Distribute the cheese over the couscous. Cover and cook over very low heat until the cheese is melted and the center is set, about 5 minutes.

Serve hot or at room temperature accompanied by the bottle of Tabasco.

OTHER IDEAS
• Before adding the cheese, set halved cherry tomatoes, cut side down, on top.
• Instead of Cheddar, use smoked Gouda, mozzarella, or jalapeño Jack.
• Add ½ to 1 cup frozen peas to the skillet when you add the couscous.

beef stir-fry with soy-spiked couscous

Seasoned couscous makes a quick and easy alternative to rice when you are serving a stir-fry. Don't be daunted because the recipe looks long. If you use the speed tips, there will be hardly any prep, and the dish is in and out of the wok in under 10 minutes.

SERVES 3 TO 4

For the stir-fry sauce

⅓ cup Japanese soy sauce (tamari or shoyu)

¼ cup dry sherry

1 tablespoon toasted sesame oil

1 tablespoon molasses

¼ to ½ teaspoon chile-garlic paste, or to taste

1 tablespoon cornstarch

For the couscous

2½ teaspoons toasted sesame oil

¼ to ½ teaspoon chile-garlic paste

1 small red bell pepper, seeded and diced

1 scallion (white and green parts), thinly sliced

1 cup whole-wheat couscous

2½ teaspoons Japanese soy sauce (tamari or shoyu), plus more to taste

¼ cup pine nuts, toasted

For the stir-fry

2½ tablespoons peanut or safflower oil

1 pound beef-top sirloin sandwich steak, cut into thin strips on the diagonal

1 large onion, halved and sliced

12 ounces shredded red cabbage (4 cups)

1 pound fresh asparagus, cut into 1-inch pieces

1 tablespoon finely chopped fresh ginger

Japanese soy sauce (tamari or shoyu), to taste

SPEED TIPS: Use presliced beef, preshredded cabbage, and a store-bought stir-fry sauce instead of the homemade one suggested in the recipe. San-J prepared sauces are quite tasty.

Make the stir-fry sauce: In a small bowl or liquid measuring cup, combine the soy sauce, sherry, ¼ cup of water, the sesame oil, molasses, chile-garlic paste, and cornstarch. Set aside.

To prepare the couscous: Warm 2 teaspoons of the sesame oil and the chile-garlic paste in a heavy 2-quart saucepan over medium heat. Stir in the bell pepper and the scallion. Cover and cook for 1 minute.

Stir in the couscous, taking care to coat the grains with the oil.

Pour 1 to 1½ cups boiling water (according to package instructions) into a glass measuring cup. Stir in the soy sauce and then stir this mixture into the couscous. Cover and let sit off the heat for 5 minutes, or until needed.

When ready to serve, stir in the remaining ½ teaspoon of sesame oil and the pine nuts as you fluff up the couscous with a fork. Add more soy sauce, if needed.

OTHER IDEAS

• **Use pork tenderloin or boneless chicken strips instead of beef.**

• **Instead of fresh asparagus, use 2 10-ounce packages defrosted frozen asparagus.**

• **Stir ½ cup roasted, salted peanuts or cashews into the stir-fry just before serving.**

• **Add 2 tablespoons chopped fresh cilantro when fluffing up the couscous.**

To prepare the stir-fry: Heat 1½ tablespoons of the peanut oil in a large wok or 12-inch skillet over high heat. Add the beef and stir-fry until the meat loses its pink color, 1 to 2 minutes. Transfer to a bowl.

Add ¼ cup of water to the wok. Add the onion and cabbage. Cover and cook over high heat until the vegetables are wilted and almost tender, about 3 minutes. Stir once or twice during this time.

Uncover, stir in the remaining tablespoon of peanut oil, the asparagus, and ginger. Continue cooking until the cabbage and asparagus are crisp-tender, 1 to 2 minutes. Add a little more water if the vegetables stick or threaten to burn.

Return the meat and any accumulated juices to the pan. Give the sauce a quick stir to reincorporate the cornstarch, and pour it over the stir-fry. Cook over medium-high heat until the sauce thickens and the beef and vegetables are glazed, another minute or two. Add more soy sauce, if needed.

To serve, make a bed of couscous on each plate. Set a portion of the stir-fry on top.

tex-mex hominy and eggs

Large kernels of hominy give scrambled eggs enough substance to move them from breakfast into the casual supper category—especially if you serve the well-seasoned mixture with warmed tortillas, sliced avocado, and some black beans tossed with a little olive oil, red onion, and cilantro.

SERVES 4

---

2 tablespoons olive oil

4 scallions, thinly sliced (keep white and green parts separate)

1 can (15 ounces) white or yellow hominy, drained and rinsed

8 large eggs

½ teaspoon granulated garlic

¼ teaspoon dried oregano

½ cup diced roasted red pepper, preferably fire-roasted

½ cup crumbled feta, plus more for serving

Salt and freshly ground black pepper

Heat the olive oil in a heavy 12-inch skillet over medium-high heat. Add the scallion whites and hominy, and cook until the scallions have softened a bit, about 2 minutes.

In a medium bowl, lightly beat the eggs with the garlic and oregano. Pour the eggs into the skillet and scatter the scallion greens, roasted red pepper, and feta on top. Scramble with a wooden spoon. Add salt and pepper to taste, and serve immediately.

OTHER IDEAS

• Stir 1 teaspoon mashed chipotle in adobo into the beaten eggs.

• Garnish with a few tablespoons of chopped fresh cilantro.

• Spoon some salsa on top of each portion, or serve salsa on the side in a bowl.

quinoa and mushroom skillet pie

The delicate vegetal taste of quinoa flakes works very well in this simple, crusty skillet pie, good for brunch, lunch, or a light supper—accompanied by a crisp green salad tossed with a lemon vinaigrette.

SERVES 3 TO 4

6 large eggs

1 cup whole milk

2 tablespoons chopped fresh parsley

1½ teaspoons salt

1 tablespoon olive oil

1 medium onion, quartered and thinly sliced

8 ounces portobello mushrooms, sliced

1 tablespoon tomato paste

1 cup quinoa flakes

1 cup frozen peas

½ cup grated sharp Cheddar cheese

SPEED TIP: Buy presliced baby 'bellos.

In a medium bowl, lightly beat the eggs. Stir in the milk, parsley, and 1 teaspoon of the salt. Set aside.

Heat the oil in a heavy 12-inch nonstick skillet that has a cover. Add the onion and cook over medium heat, stirring occasionally, until lightly browned, about 3 minutes.

Stir in the mushrooms and sprinkle with the remaining ½ teaspoon salt. Cook over high heat, stirring frequently, until the mushrooms begin to give up their liquid and soften slightly, about 3 minutes.

Stir in the tomato paste, lower the heat to medium, and continue cooking and stirring for 1 more minute. Stir in the quinoa flakes and peas. Use a spatula to evenly spread out the mixture.

Pour the egg mixture on top. As the egg becomes dry around the edges of the skillet, use a spatula to pull the cooked egg toward the center and tilt the pan to allow the uncooked egg to seep to the bottom. When the egg no longer flows to the sides, sprinkle on the cheese.

Reduce the heat to low, cover, and continue cooking until the center is set and the cheese has melted, 2 to 3 minutes. Let sit for 2 to 3 minutes before slicing and serving.

OTHER IDEAS
• Instead of Cheddar, try Gruyère, smoked mozzarella, or crumbled feta.

oat-crusted turkey cutlets with gingered cranberry relish

Oatmeal makes a crisp, tasty coating for turkey. In addition to adding oaty flavor and texture, the coating keeps the turkey moist. The cutlets make a dandy dinner accompanied by a baked sweet potato and vegetable—or try the Quinoa-Creamed Spinach (page 149). Although turkey always seems to suggest Thanksgiving, these cutlets are lovely year-round.

If you haven't yet tried using coconut oil for frying, I hope you will give it a chance. You will be amazed at the golden crust it produces without any trace of oiliness. My favorite brand is Omega Nutrition.

SERVES 4

4 turkey cutlets (about 4 ounces each)

Salt and freshly ground black pepper

⅓ cup whole-wheat flour

1 cup oatmeal (old-fashioned rolled oats)

2 teaspoons dried mint leaves

Grated zest of 1 large lemon, plus additional
    lemon zest for serving

1 large egg

1 to 2 tablespoons coconut or safflower oil

Gingered Cranberry Relish (recipe follows)

SPEED TIP: The cranberry relish is quite yummy but entirely optional—a purchased favorite makes a great stand-in, too.

Season the cutlets well on both sides with salt and pepper.

On one plate, scatter the flour. On another plate, blend the oatmeal, mint, and lemon zest. Beat the egg in a wide, shallow bowl.

Dredge each cutlet on both sides in the flour. Shake off any excess and then coat both sides with egg. Finally, coat both sides with the oat mixture, taking care to cover empty spots by pressing the oatmeal into place.

Heat 1 tablespoon of the oil in a heavy 12-inch skillet. Fry the cutlets until lightly browned and crusty on the first side, 1½ to 2 minutes. Flip and brown the second side, ½ to 1 minute. Add more oil if needed. If the cutlets are not cooked through and the coating threatens to burn, turn off the heat, cover, and let sit in the residual heat until done.

Serve with a generous portion of Gingered Cranberry Relish beside each cutlet, and pass the remaining relish in a bowl at the table.

gingered cranberry relish

It's so easy to make this cranberry relish; the entire process takes under 15 minutes. I've avoided using refined sugar by cooking the cranberries in orange juice concentrate and adding raisins. Crystallized ginger gives the relish its memorable zing. Leftovers are terrific on turkey sandwiches.

MAKES ABOUT 3½ CUPS

3 tablespoons frozen orange juice concentrate

1 pound (about 4 cups) fresh cranberries, picked over and rinsed

½ cup raisins

⅓ cup plus 2 tablespoons coarsely chopped crystallized ginger

Grated zest of 1 large orange

Honey (optional)

1 cup pecans, toasted

Blend the orange concentrate into ½ cup water in a heavy-bottomed 3-quart pot. Set over high heat. Add the cranberries, raisins, and ⅓ cup ginger.

When the liquid starts to boil, lower the heat slightly and boil uncovered, stirring occasionally, until most of the cranberries pop and the mixture thickens, 5 to 7 minutes.

Transfer the mixture to a serving bowl or glass storage container. Stir in the remaining 2 tablespoons of crystallized ginger, the orange zest, and honey to taste (if using). When the mixture has cooled, stir in the pecans. The relish can be chilled until needed, or for up to 10 days. Serve at room temperature.

quinoa-crusted chicken cutlets with cilantro pesto

Quinoa flakes are usually made into a quick morning cereal, but they have a number of other uses. You'll find them in the 10-Minute Quinoa Soup with Avocado and Corn (page 43), a Polenta-Style Quinoa (page 150), Quinoa-Creamed Spinach (page 149), and Quinoa and Mushroom Skillet Pie (page 73). In this recipe you'll discover what a delicate, crisp coating they make for chicken cutlets.

Serve the cutlets with a colorful mix of diced orange segments tossed with slices of red onion, olive oil, salt, and lime juice.

SERVES 4

4 chicken cutlets (about 4 ounces each)

Salt and freshly ground black pepper

½ cup whole-wheat pastry flour

Scant 1 cup quinoa flakes

2 teaspoons dried Italian seasoning blend

2 teaspoons Cajun seasoning blend

1 large egg

1 to 2 tablespoons coconut or safflower oil, for frying

Cilantro Pesto (recipe follows)

SPEED TIP: If you don't have time to make the Cilantro Pesto, try a store-bought pesto or olive tapenade instead.

Season the cutlets well on both sides with salt and pepper.

On one plate, scatter the flour. On another plate, blend the quinoa flakes, Italian seasoning, and Cajun seasoning. Beat the egg in a wide, shallow bowl.

Dredge each cutlet on both sides in the flour. Shake off any excess and then coat both sides with egg. Finally, fully coat both sides with the quinoa mixture, taking care to cover empty spots by pressing the quinoa flakes into place. Gently shake off any loose coating.

Heat 1 tablespoon of the oil in a heavy 12-inch skillet. Fry the cutlets until lightly browned and crusty on the first side, 1½ to 2 minutes. Flip and brown second side, 1 to 2 minutes. Add more oil if needed. If the cutlets are not cooked through and the coating threatens to burn, turn off the heat, cover, and let sit in the residual heat until done.

To serve, place a dollop of pesto on top of each cutlet and serve extra pesto in a bowl at the table.

OTHER IDEAS
- Use quinoa flakes as a coating for fish fillets.

cilantro pesto

Using cilantro instead of basil makes a nice alternative to a traditional pesto. If you clean the roots and stems well, there is no reason not to include them; they are full of flavor.

MAKES ABOUT ½ CUP

1 large bunch (4 ounces) cilantro, thoroughly
  rinsed and drained

½ cup raw pumpkin seeds

1 clove garlic, peeled

3 tablespoons olive oil

2 tablespoons freshly squeezed lime juice

½ to 1 teaspoon salt, to taste

½ teaspoon chili powder

⅓ cup pitted Spanish olives

1½ teaspoons brine from olives

Cut the bunch of cilantro in half crosswise. Place the cilantro stems and leaves in bowl of food processor. Add the pumpkin seeds and garlic, and pulse to chop. With the motor running, pour in the oil and process to create a paste.

Add the lime juice, salt, chili powder, olives, and olive brine. Pulse a few times to coarsely chop the olives. The pesto can be refrigerated for up to 3 days. Serve at room temperature.

popcorn-crusted turkey cutlets with cherry tomato salsa

Most people are surprised to learn that popcorn is a whole grain. Cooks are even more surprised to discover what a tasty coating ground popcorn makes.

Turkey cutlets cook in minutes, but the trick is to keep them from drying out. A crunchy coating made of ground, seasoned popcorn seals them beautifully, leaving the cooked meat flavorful and moist. Serve the cutlets with a mound of freshly cooked quinoa.

SERVES 4

For the cherry tomato salsa

1 pint cherry tomatoes, halved

1 cup diced roasted red bell pepper, preferably fire-roasted

1 large jalapeño, seeded and chopped

¼ cup chopped fresh cilantro

¼ cup olive oil

¼ cup finely diced red onion

2 tablespoons sherry vinegar

1 teaspoon grated lime zest

3 tablespoons freshly squeezed lime juice

¼ teaspoon salt

For the turkey cutlets

3 cups salted popped popcorn

½ teaspoon smoked Spanish or other paprika

⅛ teaspoon ground dried chipotle or cayenne

2 tablespoons whole-wheat pastry flour

1 large egg

4 turkey cutlets (about 4 ounces each)

Freshly ground black pepper

2 tablespoons coconut or safflower oil, for frying

SPEED TIP: Use a store-bought salsa, preferably a chunky, fresh one.

Make the salsa: In a medium bowl, combine the tomatoes, roasted red pepper, jalapeño, cilantro, olive oil, onion, vinegar, lime zest, lime juice, and salt. Stir well and set aside while you prepare the cutlets.

Prepare the cutlets: If there are any unpopped kernels, discard them. In several batches, grind the popcorn in a spice grinder (or do the whole batch in a food processor) to the consistency of fine bread crumbs. Set the ground popcorn on a large plate and stir in the paprika and chipotle.

Scatter the flour on another plate. Beat the egg in a medium bowl.

Season the cutlets well with pepper. Dredge them first in flour and then coat them with egg. Finally, coat them with the popcorn mixture. Shake off any loose coating.

Heat the oil in a heavy 12-inch skillet. Fry the cutlets until lightly browned and crusty on the first side, 1½ to 2 minutes. Flip and brown second side, ½ to 1 minute. If the cutlets are not cooked through and the coating threatens to burn, turn off the heat, cover, and let sit in the residual heat until done.

To serve, set a cutlet on each plate and top with salsa. Pass any extra salsa in a bowl at the table.

michael's quick brown rice with tuna and green beans

My sweetie, Michael Steinman, throws this skillet supper together when he looks up from the computer and suddenly realizes that he's ravenous.

For such moments, he always keeps a supply of Minute rice, good-quality canned tuna, and an assortment of frozen vegetables on hand to make this flash-in-the pan supper. Of course, he eats it standing up, right out of the skillet—which I don't recommend to you.

SERVES 1 TO 2

---

1 package (9 ounces) frozen cut green beans

1 can (6 ounces) tuna packed in olive oil, undrained

1 medium onion, coarsely chopped

1 teaspoon dried Italian seasoning blend

½ teaspoon granulated garlic

1 cup Minute brown rice

1 tablespoon balsamic vinegar

¼ cup coarsely chopped sun-dried tomatoes (packed in oil)

Salt and freshly ground black pepper (optional)

SPEED TIP: Double the recipe if you want to have some left over for lunch the next day.

Set the green beans in a colander and run hot water over them. Separate any that are stuck together. Set aside.

Drain the oil from the canned tuna directly into a 9-inch skillet. Set over medium-high heat and add the onion, Italian seasoning, and garlic. Cook for 1 minute.

Stir in the rice. Continue cooking, stirring occasionally, until the onion is lightly browned, 3 to 4 minutes. Add the balsamic and cook until it evaporates, about 10 seconds.

Stir in 1 cup of water and bring to a boil. Cover and cook over medium heat for 5 minutes.

Stir in the green beans and sun-dried tomatoes. Cover and cook over medium heat, stirring occasionally, until the rice is done and the green beans are tender but still firm, 3 to 5 minutes. Stir in a few tablespoons of water during this time if the mixture becomes dry.

Add the tuna to the skillet, flake it, and stir it in. Add salt and pepper to taste, if needed.

OTHER IDEAS

• Stir in ½ teaspoon chopped fennel seed with the Italian seasoning blend.

• Add a teaspoon or two of chopped capers with the tuna.

• Add some toasted, chopped walnuts or hazelnuts just before serving.

• Garnish with a few tablespoons of chopped fresh parsley.

soft chicken tacos with smoked paprika sour cream

Highly seasoned ground chicken makes a tasty filling for corn tortillas. Seasoned sour cream is the base for an irresistible sauce, giving the taco filling just the moisture it needs.

Round out the meal with a salad of diced avocado tossed with slivered red onion and endive and a lemon juice–olive oil dressing. For a heartier meal, serve spicy black beans alongside.

Allow 2 to 3 tacos per person.

MAKES 8 SOFT TACOS

For the smoked paprika sour cream

1 cup reduced-fat sour cream

1 teaspoon smoked Spanish paprika

¼ cup freshly squeezed lime juice

½ teaspoon salt, plus more to taste

For the tacos

2 tablespoons olive oil

1 cup finely diced onion

2 teaspoons chili powder

2 teaspoons dried oregano

1 teaspoon ground cumin

1 teaspoon granulated garlic

1 pound ground chicken

½ cup low-sodium chicken broth or water

1½ cups cherry tomatoes, halved or quartered (if large)

8 (6-inch) corn tortillas

OTHER IDEAS

• **Instead of ground chicken, use ground pork, beef, or turkey.**

• **Omit the oil. Chop 2 strips bacon and cook over medium heat until they render their fat and become crisp. Drain on a paper towel. Add the onion to the bacon fat and proceed as directed. Stir the crisped bacon into the chicken just before assembling the tacos.**

• **Use halved pitas or whole-wheat tortillas instead of corn tortillas.**

Make the smoked paprika sour cream: Combine the sour cream, paprika, lime juice, and salt in a bowl. Set aside.

Prepare the taco filling: In a large skillet, heat the oil over medium-high heat. Add the onion and cook, stirring frequently, until lightly browned, about 3 minutes. Toward the end of browning, stir in the chili, oregano, cumin, and garlic.

If the ground chicken has formed into a fairly solid block, cut it into small cubes. Add the chicken, broth, and half of the tomatoes to the skillet, breaking up the chicken further with a wooden spoon.

Cover and cook over medium heat until the chicken is cooked through, 2 or 3 minutes. Break up any clumps into small nuggets. Stir in the remaining cherry tomatoes and season with salt to taste.

To assemble the tacos: Heat the tortillas one by one in a skillet over medium heat, about a minute per side. Alternatively wrap all of the tortillas in a kitchen towel and heat them in the microwave for 1 minute. Set a generous ½ cup of the chicken mixture on one-half of each tortilla. Distribute about 2 tablespoons of the smoked paprika sour cream on top. Fold over and serve immediately. Repeat with remaining tortillas. Alternatively, serve the filling and sour cream in separate bowls and let each person assemble his or her own tacos at the table.

pasta
presto

Chicken, Noodles, and Snow Peas with Peanut Sauce

Penne with Cottage Cheese and Smoked Salmon

Spirals with Goat Cheese, Cherry Tomatoes, and Olives

Skillet Macaroni and Cheese with Ham and Spinach

Spirals with Beef Ragù

Fusilli with Zucchini Ribbons and Pesto

Fettuccine with Broccoli and Herbed Ricotta

Whole-Grain Shells with Halibut and Tomato Sauce

Ziti with Chicken Marsala, Mushrooms, and Fennel

Pasta Salad with Smoked Trout–Yogurt Dressing

Penne with Cucumber, Tomato, and Gorgonzola Sauce

Spaghetti with Radicchio, Arugula, and Anchovy Dressing

Pasta Frittata

chicken, noodles, and snow peas with peanut sauce

I tried this Asian-inspired dish with udon noodles and it was delicious, but I found that the udon got overcooked and mushy in a flash. Brown rice noodles retain their chewy texture and make for much tastier leftovers. In this recipe and the six that follow, you'll be cooking brown rice pasta and the sauce in the same pot. See page 24 for more details on this technique.

You can easily double this recipe, if you wish.

SERVES 4

2 tablespoons peanut or olive oil

1 pound boneless, skinless chicken breasts, cut into thin strips

8 ounces snow peas, trimmed (about 2 cups)

3 cups low-sodium chicken broth

8 ounces brown rice fettuccine

2½ tablespoons unsalted peanut butter, plus more to taste

1 tablespoon Japanese soy sauce (tamari or shoyu), plus more to taste

1 to 1½ teaspoons red curry paste, to taste

2 teaspoons Asian fish sauce

¼ cup chopped roasted peanuts (optional), for serving

SPEED TIP: Buy chicken breasts already cut up for stir-fry.

Heat the oil in a heavy 12-inch sauté pan or high-sided skillet. Add the chicken and cook over high heat, stirring frequently, until almost cooked through, 3 to 4 minutes. Stir in the snow peas and continue cooking until the chicken is done, about 2 more minutes. Transfer to a plate.

Add 2 cups of the chicken broth and 1 cup of water to the pan. Bring to a boil over high heat. Break the fettuccine in half and add it. Use a spatula to distribute the fettuccine so they are in one layer, mostly or totally submerged. Cook uncovered for 5 minutes, gently stirring from time to time. Break up any pasta that is stuck together. Toward the end of cooking, all of the pasta won't be submerged.

Meanwhile, combine the remaining 1 cup broth, the peanut butter, soy sauce, curry paste, and fish sauce. (It's okay if the sauce isn't thoroughly blended.) Stir this mixture into the pot. Taste, and blend in more peanut butter, if needed.

Cook uncovered over medium-high heat until the pasta is tender. Stir in the chicken and snow peas. Add more soy sauce, if needed. Transfer to large, shallow bowls and garnish with peanuts, if you wish. Serve immediately.

OTHER IDEAS

• Garnish with toasted sesame seeds (black are especially pretty) instead of peanuts, or add a few drops of toasted sesame oil to the peanut sauce.

• Use frozen peas instead of snow peas. Add them when you stir in the peanut sauce.

penne with cottage cheese and smoked salmon

Sliced smoked salmon makes an elegant finish to this quick pasta recipe, prepared with ingredients easily kept on hand. The cottage cheese melts down into a creamy sauce, flecked with fresh dill.

SERVES 3 TO 4

1 tablespoon unsalted butter

2 scallions, thinly sliced (keep white and green parts separate)

2 cups low-sodium chicken broth

6 ounces brown rice penne or other cut pasta (2 cups)

1 container (16 ounces) reduced-fat whipped cottage cheese or 4% small-curd cottage cheese

1 cup diced Kirby (pickling) cucumbers

1 tablespoon cornstarch (optional)

Freshly ground black pepper

¼ cup chopped fresh dill

5 to 6 ounces sliced smoked salmon

Melt the butter in a 12-inch sauté pan or high-sided skillet over medium heat. Stir in the scallion whites. Cook, stirring frequently, for 1 minute.

Gradually stir in the broth and 1½ cups of water. Bring to a rapid boil over high heat. Stir in the penne and cook uncovered for 5 minutes less than the minimum directed on the package. Stir frequently to encourage even cooking. Separate any penne that are sticking together. Toward the end of cooking, the pasta will not be completely submerged.

Reduce the heat to medium-high. Stir in the cottage cheese, cucumbers, and scallion greens. If the sauce is too thin, blend the cornstarch into 1 tablespoon of water and stir it in. Continue cooking and stirring until the sauce thickens and the pasta is al dente, about 1 minute. Season to taste with salt—keep in mind that the salmon will be salty—and pepper. Stir in the dill.

Divide into portions. Distribute a generous amount of smoked salmon on top of each portion.

OTHER IDEAS

• Omit the cucumber and instead add 1 cup frozen peas during the last minute of cooking. Just before serving, stir in 3 to 4 tablespoons chopped fresh mint. Add 1 to 2 tablespoons chopped capers along with the cucumbers.

• Add ¼ cup finely chopped red onion with the cottage cheese.

spirals with goat cheese, cherry tomatoes, and olives

In this dish a thin, creamy goat cheese sauce coats pasta spirals and fresh cherry tomatoes. If there's any sauce left at the bottom of the bowl, you'll be tempted to finish eating with a spoon.

SERVES 3 TO 4

1 tablespoon olive oil

1 tablespoon minced dried onion

¼ teaspoon dried thyme

2 cups low-sodium vegetable broth

6 ounces brown rice spirals or other cut pasta (2½ cups)

1 pint cherry tomatoes, halved

1 can (15 ounces) chickpeas, drained and rinsed

½ cup coarsely chopped, pitted olives (a mixture of green and black is nice)

2 tablespoons chopped capers

2 ounces fresh goat cheese

1 tablespoon cornstarch (optional)

2 tablespoons chopped fresh parsley

Salt and freshly ground black pepper

SPEED TIP: Use Kirby (pickling) cucumbers, which aren't waxed and don't have to be peeled.

Heat the oil in a heavy 12-inch sauté pan or deep-sided skillet over medium heat. Add the onion and thyme and cook for 10 seconds while stirring.

Gradually add the broth and 1 cup of water. Bring to a boil over high heat. Add the spirals. Cook over high heat for 5 minutes less than the minimum suggested on the package. Stir frequently to encourage even cooking. Separate any spirals that are sticking together. Toward the end of cooking, the pasta will not be completely submerged.

Stir in the tomatoes, chickpeas, olives, and capers. Cook until the pasta is just short of tender.

Reduce the heat to low. Push the pasta aside and add the goat cheese. Press a whisk into the cheese and rotate the whisk until the cheese blends into the sauce. If the sauce is too thin, blend the cornstarch into 1 tablespoon of water and stir into the pan. Stir well and cook until the sauce thickens, 1 to 2 minutes. Add the parsley and salt and pepper to taste. Serve immediately or continue cooking until the pasta is al dente, another minute or two.

OTHER IDEAS
- Use black beans instead of chickpeas.
- Try chopped dill or cilantro instead of parsley.

skillet macaroni and cheese with ham and spinach

Ham and spinach supplement the classic mac-and-cheese combo, grounding it firmly in the main-dish dinner category. They also add very pretty specks of color.

In theory, this amount of pasta should serve 5 or 6 people, but there is something about macaroni and cheese that makes it impossible to eat only one portion, so play it safe and figure on feeding four. Then enjoy the leftovers, if there are any.

SERVES 4

2 cups low-sodium chicken broth

9 ounces brown rice elbows (3 cups)

5 ounces smoked ham steak, cut into ¼-inch dice (1 scant cup)

2¼ packed cups grated extra-sharp Cheddar cheese (10 ounces)

Salt and freshly ground black pepper

1 tablespoon cornstarch (optional)

1 package (10 ounces) prewashed fresh spinach, chopped

Combine the broth and 2½ cups of water in a 12-inch sauté pan or deep-sided skillet and bring to a rapid boil over high heat. Stir in the pasta and boil uncovered for 3 minutes less than the minimum directed on the package. Stir frequently to encourage even cooking. Separate any pasta that sticks together. Toward the end of cooking, the pasta will not be completely submerged.

Reduce the heat to medium-high. Stir in the ham and cheese. Add salt, if needed, and pepper to taste.

If there is an abundance of thin sauce at this point, blend the cornstarch into 1 tablespoon of water in a small bowl. Stir the cornstarch slurry into the pot.

Stir in the spinach. Continue cooking uncovered, stirring frequently, until the pasta is al dente and the sauce is creamy and thick, 1 to 3 minutes. If the sauce becomes thick before the pasta is tender, turn off the heat and cover the pot for a minute or two.

Transfer to large, shallow bowls. Grate lots of fresh pepper on top of each portion.

OTHER IDEAS

• Stir in ¼ teaspoon or more prepared mustard at the end.
• Garnish each serving with snipped chives.
• For a Tex-Mex twist: Use half Monterey pepper Jack and half Cheddar. A few minutes before the pasta is done, stir in some halved cherry tomatoes, 1 teaspoon mashed chipotle in adobo, and about ¼ cup chopped, pitted black olives. Garnish each portion with chopped fresh cilantro.
• For an Italian twist: Use smoked mozzarella Instead of Cheddar and chopped prosciutto instead of ham. Add chopped fresh basil and about ¼ cup chopped, oil-soaked, sun-dried tomatoes at the end. Garnish each serving with grated Parmesan cheese.

spirals with beef ragù

If you have the idea that pasta with a homemade meat sauce requires several pots and a few hours in the kitchen, this recipe will change your mind. Using only a large skillet, you'll be making a quick, flavor-packed meaty tomato sauce and then cooking the pasta right in the sauce. The pasta develops complex flavor as it cooks, absorbing liquid and simultaneously thickening the sauce.

Spirals are a particularly nice shape to use for this dish since little bits of flavorful beef get caught in the crevices. Diced zucchini added toward the end provides contrasting texture, but what makes this dish particularly memorable is the garnish of crumbled feta, lemon zest, and chopped rosemary sprinkled on top just before serving.

SERVES 4 TO 6

---

2 tablespoons olive oil

1½ cups coarsely chopped onion

1 pound ground beef

1 teaspoon dried thyme

½ teaspoon granulated garlic

3 tablespoons tomato paste

⅓ cup dry red or white wine or vermouth

2 cups low-sodium chicken broth

1 can (28 ounces) diced tomatoes, with liquid

Salt

9 ounces brown rice fusilli or other cut pasta
    (3 cups)

1 medium to large zucchini, cut into ½-inch dice (2 cups)

Freshly ground black pepper

Pinch of sugar (optional)

⅓ cup crumbled feta

Grated zest of 1 large lemon

1 tablespoon finely chopped fresh rosemary

OTHER IDEAS

• **Use ground lamb, pork, chicken, or turkey instead of beef.**
• **Add 1 to 2 teaspoons chopped fresh oregano just before serving.**
• **Refrigerate overnight and serve the next day as a room-temperature salad. Perk up with a little fresh lemon juice.**
• **Substitute penne or orecchiette for the spirals.**

Heat the oil in a heavy 12-inch sauté pan or high-sided skillet over medium-high heat. Add the onion and cook until it is lightly browned, 3 to 5 minutes.

Add the beef, thyme, and garlic. Continue cooking until the meat loses its pink color, breaking up blocks into small bits as you go. Stir in the tomato paste and cook while stirring for another minute.

Stir in the wine and cook until it evaporates, about 1 minute. Add the broth, 1½ cups of water, tomatoes, and 1 teaspoon salt. Bring to a rapid boil over high heat. Stir in the pasta.

Cook over high heat for 5 minutes. The pasta will not be completely submerged toward the end of cooking, so stir frequently to promote even cooking and to prevent the pasta from sticking to the bottom of the skillet. Break up any pasta that is sticking together.

Stir in the zucchini and add pepper to taste. Add sugar, if needed, to balance the acidity of the tomatoes.

Continue boiling over high heat, stirring from time to time, until the pasta is done. If the sauce becomes thick before the pasta is ready, turn off the heat, cover, and let sit until the pasta is tender, but still firm, usually no more than a minute or two.

In a small bowl, combine the feta, lemon zest, and rosemary.

To serve, ladle into large, shallow bowls. Sprinkle the feta mixture on top.

fusilli with zucchini ribbons and pesto

This pretty dish is made by peeling zucchini and carrots into ribbons, then barely cooking the ribbons with the pasta at the very end.

SERVES 4

2 cups low-sodium vegetable broth

9 ounces brown rice fusilli or other cut pasta (3 cups)

2 large zucchini (about 1½ pounds), trimmed

1 large carrot, trimmed

3 to 4 tablespoons store-bought basil pesto, to taste

½ cup walnuts, toasted and coarsely chopped

2 to 3 tablespoons grated Parmesan cheese, to taste, plus more for serving

Grated zest of 1 large lemon

Salt and freshly ground black pepper

In a heavy 12-inch sauté pan or high-sided skillet, bring the broth and 2 cups of water to a rapid boil. Add the penne. Cook over high heat, stirring frequently to prevent sticking, for 1 minute less than the shortest cooking time suggested by the package instructions. Stir frequently to encourage even cooking. Separate any pasta that sticks together. Toward the end of cooking, the pasta will not be completely submerged.

While the pasta is cooking, make the zucchini and carrot ribbons: Balancing the zucchini at an angle, use a peeler and moderate pressure along the length to make the first strip. Position the peeler blade so that remaining strips will have a thin dark green strip on one side. Continue peeling the plain white flesh until you reach the seeds; toss. Repeat with the carrot until you get too close to the core to continue.

When the pasta is a fraction short of done, add the zucchini and carrot strips and cook for 30 seconds. If there is a lot of unabsorbed water, tilt the pot and spoon some off, leaving about ½ cup liquid in the pot.

Turn off the heat. Stir in the pesto, walnuts, cheese, and lemon zest. Add salt and pepper to taste. Divide into portions and garnish with additional cheese.

fettuccine with broccoli and herbed ricotta

Here's my light, whole-grain version of pasta primavera.

SERVES 2 TO 3

4 cups fresh broccoli florets

2 cups low-sodium chicken or vegetable broth

8 ounces brown rice fettuccine

1 teaspoon dried oregano

¼ to ½ teaspoon crushed red pepper flakes, to taste

½ teaspoon salt

2 cups reduced-fat ricotta

½ cup chopped sun-dried tomatoes (packed in oil)

¼ cup grated Parmesan cheese, plus more for serving

2 to 3 teaspoons chopped fresh rosemary

Freshly ground black pepper

SPEED TIP: Use a 1-pound package of frozen broccoli florets, or buy the cut florets at a salad bar.

In a heavy 12-inch sauté pan or high-sided skillet, bring 1 cup of water to a rapid boil over high heat. Add the broccoli, cover, and steam until crisp-tender, about 3 minutes. Drain and run under cold water. Set the broccoli aside.

In the same pan, bring the broth and 2 cups of water to a boil over high heat.

Stir in the fettuccine, oregano, red pepper flakes, and salt. Cook uncovered for 3 minutes less than the minimum directed on the package. Stir frequently to encourage even cooking. Separate any fettuccine that are sticking together. Toward the end of cooking, the pasta will not be completely submerged.

Reduce the heat to medium-high. Push the pasta to one side of the skillet. Blend the ricotta and sun-dried tomatoes into the broth. Continue cooking and stirring until the sauce thickens and the pasta is al dente, 2 to 3 minutes more. If the sauce becomes quite thick before the pasta is done, cover the pot and let it sit off the heat for a minute or two.

Stir in the Parmesan, rosemary, additional salt, if needed, and pepper to taste. Serve in large bowls, sprinkled with a little more Parmesan.

whole-grain shells with halibut and tomato sauce

Whip up a quick homemade tomato sauce dotted with olives and capers, and steam halibut fillets on top. Toss pasta shells into the sauce for a meal that will transport your taste buds to the south of France.

SERVES 4

4 halibut fillets (4 to 6 ounces each)

Salt and freshly ground black pepper

2 tablespoons olive oil

1 large onion, coarsely chopped

1 large clove garlic, minced

1 teaspoon fennel seeds, chopped

½ cup dry red or white wine

1 can (28 ounces) diced tomatoes, with liquid

½ cup pitted black olives, preferably oil-cured, coarsely chopped

¼ cup brined capers, coarsely chopped

½ teaspoon salt

Freshly ground black pepper

9 ounces whole-grain shells or other cut pasta (3 cups)

¼ cup chopped fresh parsley

OTHER IDEAS

• Rather than halibut, use other firm-fleshed fillets, such as scrod or pompano.

• Instead of wine, use ⅓ cup Pernod.

• Add ½ teaspoon crushed red pepper flakes along with the fennel seeds.

• Use half green olives and half black olives, or double the total amount of olives.

• Add orange zest to the sauce after cooking the halibut.

SPEED TIP: Buy black oil-cured olives that are already pitted.

Season the fillets on both sides with salt and pepper. Set aside. Bring a large pot of salted water to a boil.

Meanwhile, heat the oil in a heavy, nonreactive skillet large enough to hold the fillets in one layer. Add the onion and cook over medium-high heat, stirring frequently, until lightly browned, about 4 minutes. Add the garlic and fennel seeds, and cook an additional minute. Stir in the wine and cook until most of it evaporates, about 1 minute.

Stir in the tomatoes, olives, capers, ½ teaspoon salt, and a few twists of pepper. Bring to a boil. Reduce the heat and simmer uncovered, stirring occasionally, until the flavors mingle, about 10 minutes. Adjust the seasonings.

Add the pasta to the boiling water.

Set the halibut fillets on top of the sauce, cover, and raise the heat to medium high. Cook until the fish turns opaque, 4 to 5 minutes, depending on thickness. Remove the cover and turn off the heat. Spoon some of the sauce on top of the fish.

When the pasta is just short of done, drain it, reserving about 1 cup of the pasta water. Transfer the halibut to a platter. Stir the pasta and 3 tablespoons of the parsley into the sauce. If the sauce seems too thick, thin it by stirring in some of the reserved pasta water. Continue cooking until the pasta is done, 1 to 2 minutes longer.

To serve, divide the pasta among four plates and set the halibut on top. Garnish the halibut with the remaining parsley and serve immediately.

ziti with chicken marsala, mushrooms, and fennel

On a recent trip to Sicily, I visited the town of Marsala and became intrigued with the idea of using the region's wine in cooking. Marsala adds a hint of fruity sweetness that is perfect for chicken. No wonder Chicken Marsala has become such a classic dish.

In this skillet pasta recipe, I've used Marsala to add an interesting layer of flavor in a quickly prepared sauce. The sauce is loaded with mushrooms, giving it an earthy depth. Chopped fresh fennel is something you might not expect to find in this dish, but I tried it on a whim and was completely won over by how much good taste and texture it added.

SERVES 4

1 pound boneless, skinless chicken breasts

Salt and freshly ground black pepper

1 medium bulb fennel

9 ounces whole-grain ziti or other cut pasta (3 cups)

2 tablespoons olive oil

8 ounces cremini or button mushrooms, sliced

1 teaspoon fennel seeds, chopped

½ cup Marsala

1 cup low-sodium chicken broth

1 tablespoon cornstarch

OTHER IDEAS

• Use turkey cutlets instead of chicken.

• Use dry sherry instead of Marsala.

• Leave out the fennel bulb and seeds, and add 1 teaspoon dried tarragon when you add the Marsala.

• If the fennel has no fronds, use 3 tablespoons chopped fresh parsley or 2 teaspoons chopped fresh tarragon.

SPEED TIP: Buy presliced chicken for the stir-fry.

Cut the chicken into strips about 2 inches long and ½ inch wide. Season well with salt and pepper. Set aside.

Snip off and chop the leafy fronds of the fennel. Slice off and discard the stalks or reserve them for stock. Cut the bulb in half. Slice away the V-shaped inner core and thinly slice the bulbs lengthwise.

Bring a large pot of salted water to a boil. Add the ziti and cook according to package directions until just short of tender. Start checking for doneness a few minutes early to avoid overcooking.

Meanwhile, heat the oil in a heavy 12-inch nonstick skillet or sauté pan over high heat. Add the mushrooms, fennel, and fennel seeds, and season with salt. Cook, stirring frequently, until the mushrooms shrivel and give up most of their liquid, about 3 minutes.

Stir in the chicken and continue cooking, stirring constantly, until the chicken turns white, about 1 minute. Add the Marsala and cook until about half evaporates, 1 to 2 minutes.

Stir in the broth and bring to a gentle boil. Add salt and pepper to taste. Cover and cook until the chicken is cooked through, 1 to 3 minutes.

Meanwhile, in a small bowl blend the cornstarch with 1 tablespoon of water. Stir the cornstarch slurry into the skillet and cook over medium-high heat while stirring until the mixture thickens, a minute or two.

When the pasta is done, drain it. Stir it into the chicken mixture. Garnish with the fennel fronds.

pasta salad with smoked trout–yogurt dressing

Smoked trout is so full of flavor that it takes little else to create a simple but distinctive dressing for a pasta salad. Here I use a low-fat yogurt base and add a generous amount of parsley. Tossing in lots of shredded Romaine lightens the mix and gives it some crunch—perfect for a light supper on a warm evening.

SERVES 2 TO 3

Salt

8 ounces whole-grain shells or other cut pasta

1 cup low-fat yogurt

2 to 4 teaspoons prepared horseradish, to taste

2 tablespoons chopped capers

6 to 7 ounces smoked trout, coarsely chopped
    (1 generous cup)

2 cups cherry tomatoes, halved

⅓ cup chopped fresh parsley

6 cups shredded Romaine

Bring a large pot of salted water to a rolling boil. Add the pasta and cook according to package directions until done. Start checking for doneness about 5 minutes before the end of suggested cooking time to avoid overcooking.

While the pasta is cooking, prepare the sauce: In a large bowl, blend the yogurt, 2 teaspoons of horseradish, and the capers. Stir in the smoked trout. Add more horseradish, if needed.

When the pasta is al dente, drain it and run it under cold water to cool. Drain well. Toss the pasta, tomatoes, and parsley into the yogurt sauce. Just before serving, gently toss in the Romaine.

OTHER IDEAS
- **Use smoked mackerel instead of trout.**
- **Add about ¼ cup minced red onion or thinly sliced scallions.**

Squash Bisque with Curried Popcorn, page 41

Soba Noodle Soup with Asian Vegetables and Shrimp, page 47

Fruity-Nutty Wild Rice and Turkey Salad, page 139

Fusilli with Zucchini Ribbons and Pesto, page 90

Oat-Crusted Turkey Cutlets with Gingered Cranberry Relish, pages 74–75
Quinoa-Creamed Spinach, page 149

Quinoa Paella with Chicken and Chorizo, page 114

Hominy and Kidney Bean Chili, page 51
Southwestern Mini-Loaves, page 169

Skillet Macaroni and Cheese with Ham and Spinach, page 87

Soft Chicken Tacos with Smoked Paprika Sour Cream, pages 80–81

Bean-Chorizo Tortilla Stack, page 124
Buckwheat with Cheddar and Pickled Jalapeños, page 144

Beef Stir-Fry with Soy-Spiked Couscous, pages 70–71

Torticotti, page 129

Michael's Quick Brown Rice with Tuna and Green Beans, page 79

Berry-Orange Pancakes, page 165

Fresh Fruit–Topped Cake, pages 196–197

penne with cucumber, tomato, and gorgonzola sauce

Coat penne, chopped cucumbers, and cherry tomatoes with a creamy, flavorful, no-cook Gorgonzola cheese sauce—a good choice for busy cooks on a hot summer's day. I've kept the recipe fairly low in fat by mixing the Gorgonzola with yogurt.

Serve hot or as a room-temperature pasta salad.

SERVES 5 TO 6

Salt

1 pound whole-grain penne (5 cups)

5 to 6 ounces Gorgonzola, crumbled or chopped into bits

2 cups low-fat or fat-free plain yogurt, preferably Greek-style

3 cups sliced cucumber, preferably Persian or Kirby

2 cups halved cherry tomatoes or chopped plum tomatoes

2 tablespoons olive oil

Freshly ground black pepper

2 to 3 teaspoons balsamic vinegar, to taste

3 tablespoons chopped fresh parsley

Bring a large pot of salted water to a boil. Add the penne and cook according to package directions until just short of tender. Start checking for doneness a few minutes early to avoid overcooking.

Meanwhile, in a large bowl, stir together the Gorgonzola and yogurt, but don't blend until smooth—it's nice to leave little crumbles of Gorgonzola intact.

When the pasta is tender but firm, drain it, reserving about 1 cup of the water.

Add the pasta to the bowl. Stir in the cucumbers, tomatoes, and olive oil. Toss well. Stir in a little of the reserved pasta water if the yogurt mixture is too thick to distribute easily. Season with salt and pepper. Add balsamic to pick up the flavors. Garnish with the parsley.

OTHER IDEAS

• Use a domestic blue cheese instead of imported Gorgonzola.

• Try dill or mint instead of parsley.

spaghetti with radicchio, arugula, and anchovy dressing

I made this dish one day when all I had in the fridge was some interesting salad ingredients. It turned out to be a keeper: lovely on its own and also good with grilled fish.

SERVES 4

Salt

8 ounces whole-grain spaghetti

5 tablespoons olive oil

3 tablespoons freshly squeezed lemon juice

1 teaspoon anchovy paste

5 to 6 tablespoons grated Romano cheese, to taste, plus more for serving

2 bunches arugula (about 12 ounces total), chopped, including stems

6 ounces radicchio, cut into thin slivers

Freshly ground black pepper

SPEED TIP: Use 1 pound of prewashed salad greens instead of the radicchio and arugula.

Bring a large pot of salted water to a boil. Add the spaghetti and cook according to package directions until just short of tender. Start checking for doneness a few minutes early to avoid overcooking.

While the pasta is cooking, prepare the dressing in a large bowl by whisking together the oil, lemon juice, anchovy paste, and Romano cheese.

When the pasta is done, drain it, reserving about 1 cup of the water.

Toss the pasta, arugula, and radicchio into the dressing, adding enough of the pasta water to make the dressing slightly creamy. Add pepper to taste, and more Romano cheese, if needed. Garnish individual portions with extra cheese.

OTHER IDEAS
• Use watercress instead of arugula and red cabbage instead of radicchio.

pasta frittata

Recently I found myself with a few cups of leftover pasta and had fun incorporating it into a quick and tasty stove-top frittata. The pasta was lightly sauced—not enough to give the frittata good flavor—so I seasoned the eggs well by stirring in a little salsa.

Serve slices of the frittata with a big salad for lunch or a casual supper. It's also good cold with an extra dollop of salsa on top.

SERVES 3 TO 4

4 large eggs, lightly beaten

½ to ⅓ cup chunky salsa or tomato sauce, to taste (optional)

¼ teaspoon salt, or to taste

Freshly ground black pepper

2 tablespoons olive oil

2 to 3 cups cooked whole-grain pasta (chop long pasta into 2-inch bits)

¼ cup grated sharp Cheddar cheese

In a small bowl, lightly beat the eggs. Stir in the salsa if the pasta isn't flavorfully sauced. Season with salt and pepper.

Heat the oil in an 8- or 9-inch skillet over medium-high heat.

Scatter the pasta in the skillet. Pour the eggs over the top and immediately begin lifting up the pasta around the perimeter so that the eggs can seep underneath. Continue doing this until there is very little runny egg in the center, 3 to 5 minutes. Lower the heat if necessary.

Distribute the cheese on top. Cover and cook over very low heat until the cheese is melted and the center is set, about 3 more minutes.

Uncover and let it sit off the heat for a few minutes before cutting into wedges to serve.

OTHER IDEAS

• Add chopped, pitted olives with the salsa.

• Use crumbled feta or goat cheese or grated smoked Gouda instead of the Cheddar.

• Stir finely chopped, cooked vegetables or frozen peas into the pasta before adding the eggs.

• Fry a few slices of salami before adding oil to the skillet. Chop and distribute on top before adding the cheese.

stove-top
casseroles
and pilaf
entrées

Barley with Mushrooms, Beef, and Dill Sour Cream

Curried Barley and Beef with Mango Chutney Yogurt

Bulgur with Lamb, Beans, Feta, Mint, and Lemon

Lamb Chops with Bulgur Pilaf

Farro Risotto with Pancetta, Asparagus, and Hazelnuts

Farro with Broccoli Rabe and Prosciutto

Farro with Italian Sausage, Escarole, and Sun-Dried Tomatoes

Lamb with Millet and Mint-Cucumber Salad

Millet with Collards and Ham

    Millet Casserole

Quinoa Paella with Chicken and Chorizo

Coconut Chicken Curry with Thai Black Rice

Curried Brown Rice with Smoked Trout

Chili Brown Rice with Chicken, Black Beans, and Olives

barley with mushrooms, beef, and dill sour cream

When you think of barley, mushrooms, and beef, a steaming bowl of homey soup comes to mind, but in this recipe I've put them together in a dish that is more like a pilaf. Adding a touch of sour cream at the last minute coats the barley and gives the mixture a rich, creamy finish.

SERVES 4

1 pound cremini or button mushrooms

1 pound beef pepper steak, thinly sliced

Salt and freshly ground black pepper

2 tablespoons olive oil

1 medium onion, coarsely chopped

1 teaspoon smoked Spanish paprika or other
    paprika

5 cups low-sodium beef or chicken broth, plus
    more if needed

3 cups quick-cooking barley

1 cup reduced-fat sour cream

¼ cup plus 2 tablespoons chopped fresh dill,
    plus a few sprigs for garnish

Grated zest of 1 lemon

1 tablespoon freshly squeezed lemon juice

Use a damp paper towel to wipe any dirt from the mushrooms. Slice large mushrooms in half and then cut each half into ¼-inch slices. Quarter small mushrooms. Set aside.

Season the beef with salt and pepper. Heat 1 tablespoon of the oil in a heavy 3-quart Dutch oven over high heat. Add the beef and cook, stirring frequently, just until it loses its pink color, about 1 minute. Transfer the beef to a bowl.

Add the mushrooms to the pot. Sprinkle with ¼ teaspoon salt. Lower the heat slightly, and cook while stirring until they are lightly browned, but not thoroughly cooked, about 1 minute. Transfer to the bowl holding the beef.

Heat the remaining tablespoon oil in the pot. Add the onion and cook over medium heat, stirring occasionally until lightly browned, about 2 minutes. Stir in the paprika and cook for another minute.

Add the broth and bring it to a boil over high heat. Stir in the barley, cover, and cook over medium-high heat for 5 minutes.

Meanwhile, cut the beef into bite-sized pieces. After the barley has cooked for 5 minutes, stir in the mushrooms, beef, and any accumulated juices.

Cover and simmer until the barley is tender (it will remain a little chewy), about 5 minutes longer. Stir in ½ cup of the sour cream and the 2 tablespoons dill. Add salt and pepper to taste.

OTHER IDEAS

• **Use shiitake or oyster mushrooms in place of some or all of the cremini.**

• **Use ground beef or pork instead of pepper steak.**

• **Add 1 cup frozen peas when you stir in the sour cream.**

In a small bowl, stir together the remaining ½ cup sour cream, the remaining ¼ cup of dill, and the lemon zest and juice.

Set a generous tablespoon of dilled sour cream on top of each portion and garnish with sprigs of dill.

curried barley and beef with mango chutney yogurt

Beef adds depth of flavor to this simply prepared pilaf. The unusual topping—made by combining mango chutney and yogurt—gives it an intriguing, slightly sweet finish.

SERVES 4

---

1 tablespoon olive oil

1 pound ground beef

1 teaspoon salt

1 medium onion, finely chopped

1 tablespoon mild Madras curry powder

1 teaspoon ground cumin

1 cup quick-cooking barley

1 package (10 ounces) frozen cut green beans

1 heaping tablespoon sweet mango chutney

1 cup plain low-fat yogurt

¼ cup chopped fresh cilantro

Heat the oil in a heavy 3-quart Dutch oven over medium-high heat. Add the beef and sprinkle on ¼ teaspoon of the salt. Cook, breaking up any chunks with a large spoon, until most of the meat is no longer pink, about 4 minutes.

Stir in the onion, curry powder, and cumin, and cook until the onion begins to soften, 2 to 3 minutes.

Add 2 cups of water and the remaining ¾ teaspoon of salt. Bring to a boil. Add the barley. Cover and cook over medium heat for 5 minutes.

Meanwhile, set the green beans in a strainer and run them under hot water to break up the block and partially defrost. Drain well.

Stir the green beans into the barley. Cover and cook over medium heat for 4 minutes. Turn off the heat and let the mixture sit until the barley and green beans are tender, 3 to 5 more minutes.

In a small bowl combine the chutney, yogurt, and cilantro. Make a mound of the curried barley on each plate. Spoon a few tablespoons of mango chutney yogurt on top of each portion. Serve extra mango chutney yogurt in a small bowl on the side.

OTHER IDEAS
- Use ground lamb or pork instead of beef.
- Add a pinch of cayenne pepper along with the curry powder.
- Toast 1 tablespoon black mustard seeds and stir them in with the green beans.

bulgur with lamb, beans, feta, mint, and lemon

Based on a traditional combination of ingredients, this hearty casserole offers a variety of tastes and textures, all united by the wake-up topping of salty feta tossed with lots of mint and lemon zest.

SERVES 4 TO 6

1 cup crumbled feta

¼ cup chopped fresh mint

2 teaspoons grated lemon zest

1 tablespoon freshly squeezed lemon juice

2 tablespoons olive oil

8 ounces ground lamb

2 tablespoons minced dried onion

1½ teaspoons dried oregano

1 teaspoon granulated garlic

Salt and freshly ground black pepper

2 tablespoons tomato paste

3 tablespoons balsamic vinegar

½ cup coarse bulgur

½ cup brown rice elbows or other small cut pasta

1 cup kalamata olives (pitting optional)

3 to 4 medium zucchini (1¾ pounds), quartered lengthwise and cut into 1-inch chunks

½ cup roasted red bell pepper, preferably fire-roasted, cut into 1-inch pieces

1 can (15 ounces) cannellini beans, drained and rinsed

In a medium bowl, toss together the feta, mint, lemon zest, and juice. Set aside.

In a heavy 4-quart Dutch oven, heat the oil over medium-high heat. Add the lamb, onion, oregano, garlic, and salt and pepper to taste. Brown the meat, stirring well to break up any chunks, about 3 minutes. Turn the heat down to medium. Stir in the tomato paste and cook another minute. Stir in the balsamic vinegar and cook until it evaporates, about 30 seconds.

Add 2 cups of water and bring to a boil. Add the bulgur, cover, and cook over medium heat for 10 minutes. Check the cooking time of your pasta. If it takes longer than 10 minutes, stir it in at this time and cook covered for the extra minutes required before stirring in the olives and zucchini. Cover and continue cooking, stirring occasionally, until the bulgur, pasta, and zucchini are tender, about 10 more minutes. Adjust the seasonings. Stir in the roasted red pepper and beans, and cook for a minute or two until they are hot.

To serve, divide among the plates and scatter a tablespoon or two of the feta mixture on top. Serve the remaining feta in a bowl at the table.

OTHER IDEAS

- Add a clove of minced garlic to the feta topping.
- Use parsley instead of mint in the feta topping, or add 2 or 3 tablespoons parsley in addition to the mint.

lamb chops with bulgur pilaf

Most people are familiar with fine bulgur—the kind used to make tabbouleh. While fine bulgur needs only a brief soak in hot water, the coarse bulgur used in this pilaf requires about 20 minutes of cooking to become tender. It's worth the wait since coarse bulgur has more character than the fine grind and a very pleasing chewiness.

Bulgur is a staple grain in Turkey, where pilafs are often colored with a bit of tomato paste and dotted with raisins, as I've done here. For a quickly assembled duo, try some spice-coated, skillet-fried lamb chops alongside the pilaf. A sprightly tossed salad that includes chopped fresh mint leaves makes an ideal accompaniment.

SERVES 4

For the pilaf

2 tablespoons olive oil

½ cup chopped onion

1½ tablespoons tomato paste

1½ cups coarse bulgur

½ cup raisins

1 teaspoon salt

For the chops

1 teaspoon salt

1 teaspoon smoked Spanish paprika or other paprika

½ teaspoon ground cumin

½ teaspoon freshly ground black pepper

4 shoulder lamb chops, about ½-inch thick

2 tablespoons olive oil

¼ cup slivered almonds, toasted, for garnish

OTHER IDEAS

• In the pilaf, use dried cranberries or cherries instead of raisins.

• Stir canned, drained chickpeas into the pilaf just after adding the water.

• Add ½ teaspoon dried crumbled mint to the pilaf when you add the water.

• Use one of your favorite dry meat rubs instead of the seasoning blend.

• Garnish with roasted salted pistachios instead of almonds.

• If pomegranates are in season, sprinkle the ruby-red seeds over the pilaf and chops for a dramatic finish.

Make the pilaf: In a heavy 3-quart Dutch oven, heat the oil over medium-high heat. Add the onion and cook, stirring occasionally, until lightly browned, 2 to 3 minutes. Stir in the tomato paste and continue cooking, stirring constantly, for 20 seconds.

Stir in the bulgur. Lower the heat to medium and stir to thoroughly coat the bulgur with the tomato paste, about 1 minute.

Stir in 3 cups of water, taking care to scrape up any browned bits on the bottom of the pot. Add the raisins and salt. Cover and bring to a boil over high heat. Reduce the heat to low and cook until most or all of the water has been absorbed, about 20 minutes. Turn off the heat and let steam until the bulgur is tender, 5 to 10 minutes, or until needed.

While the bulgur is cooking, prepare the lamb chops: In a small bowl, blend the salt, paprika, cumin, and pepper. Sprinkle the seasoning onto both sides of the chops, and rub it into the meat.

Heat the oil in a heavy skillet large enough to hold all of the chops. Cook over high heat until well browned on the first side, 6 to 8 minutes. Turn and brown on second side until cooked to desired doneness, 3 to 5 minutes for medium rare, and a few more minutes for medium.

To serve, make a bed of pilaf and set one lamb chop per person on top. Garnish with almonds.

farro risotto with pancetta, asparagus, and hazelnuts

Farro makes a lovely risotto. In fact, the Italians have a special name for it: farrotto. This farrotto is dotted with diced pancetta, an Italian bacon that is salt-cured rather than smoked like American bacon.

Farrotto is not as creamy as risottos made with Arborio or other short-grain white rices, but it has a lovely nutty flavor and a pleasing chewiness somewhat like barley.

SERVES 4

1 pound asparagus, trimmed

2 teaspoons olive oil

2 ounces pancetta, finely diced (about ⅓ cup)

⅓ cup finely chopped shallots or onion

1 cup semi-pearled farro

⅓ cup dry white wine or vermouth

1 quart low-sodium chicken broth

Salt

1 cup shredded radicchio

½ cup hazelnuts, toasted and coarsely chopped

¼ cup Parmesan cheese, plus more for serving

Freshly ground black pepper

Cut off the asparagus tips. Slice the stems about ¼ inch thick. Set the tips and stems aside.

Heat the oil in a heavy 4-quart Dutch oven over medium-high heat. Stir in the pancetta and cook, stirring frequently, until lightly browned and crisp, 2 to 3 minutes. Remove with a slotted spoon and set on paper towels to drain.

Add the shallots to the pot and cook, stirring occasionally, for 1 minute. Stir in the farro, reduce the heat slightly, and stir to coat. Continue cooking until the farro is lightly toasted and starts to pop, 2 to 3 minutes.

Stir in the wine and cook until it evaporates, about 30 seconds. Stir in 1 cup of the broth and boil, uncovered, over medium-high heat until the farro has absorbed most of the liquid, about 10 minutes.

Meanwhile, heat the remaining 3 cups broth in a second pot. When it comes to a boil, reduce the heat to low. Gradually stir the remaining broth into the farro, a cup at a time, adding more as the mixture becomes dry. Stir frequently during this phase, which should take 10 to 15 minutes.

When you add the last cup of broth, add the asparagus and salt to taste. Raise the heat to high. Cook, stirring almost constantly, for 3 minutes. Add the radicchio and continue cooking and stirring until the liquid thickens and the asparagus and farro are tender, about 5 minutes longer.

Turn off the heat. Stir in the crisped pancetta, hazelnuts, Parmesan, and pepper to taste. Serve extra Parmesan in a small bowl at the table.

farro with broccoli rabe and prosciutto

Farro, an ancient cousin to wheat, is much beloved by Italians for good reason: It cooks quickly and is quite versatile. An added boon is that farro doesn't get hard (the way rice does) when refrigerated, so leftovers can easily be served as a room-temperature salad.

SERVES 4 TO 6

2 tablespoons olive oil

1 tablespoon minced dried onion

1 teaspoon dried Italian seasoning blend

1 teaspoon granulated garlic

¼ teaspoon crushed red pepper flakes

1¼ cups semi-pearled farro

2 cups low-sodium chicken broth

1 large bunch broccoli rabe (about 1 pound)

4 ounces thinly sliced prosciutto, chopped

Salt and freshly ground black pepper

1 to 2 teaspoons balsamic vinegar, to taste
   (optional)

Heat 1 tablespoon of the oil in a heavy 4-quart Dutch oven over medium-high heat. Stir in the onion, Italian seasoning, garlic, and red pepper flakes. Cook while stirring for 30 seconds. Stir in the farro.

Gradually stir in the broth and 1 cup of water. Bring to a boil. Cover and cook over medium heat for 15 minutes.

Meanwhile, prepare the broccoli rabe: Holding the stalks in a bunch, trim off and discard the bottom inch of the stems. Slice the remaining stems about ½ inch thick. Coarsely chop the leaves, trying to leave small florets whole.

After the farro has cooked for 15 minutes, stir in the broccoli rabe. (If it doesn't all fit at once, add half, cover and steam until wilted, about 1 minute. Then add the rest.) Cover and continue cooking until the broccoli rabe and farro are tender, 4 to 6 minutes. Add a bit more water if the mixture becomes dry before the dish is done.

Stir in the prosciutto and remaining tablespoon oil. Add salt and pepper to taste. Stir in a little balsamic vinegar, if needed, to sharpen the flavors.

OTHER IDEAS
• **Substitute broccoli florets and chopped stems for the broccoli rabe.**
• **Garnish each portion with a light dusting of grated Parmesan cheese.**
• **Add a little olive oil and lemon juice and serve at room temperature on a bed of shredded radicchio.**

farro with italian sausage, escarole, and sun-dried tomatoes

A satisfying mélange of classic Italian ingredients, this pilaf-like dish has a long-cooked taste that belies the ease of preparation.

SERVES 4

1 tablespoon olive oil

12 ounces fresh Italian sausage

2 cups low-sodium chicken or beef broth, plus more if needed

2 cups semi-pearled farro

½ teaspoon crushed red pepper flakes (if sausage isn't hot)

¼ cup chopped sun-dried tomatoes packed in oil

1½ pounds escarole, chopped

Grated zest of 1 large lemon

Salt and freshly ground black pepper

Heat the oil in a heavy 4-quart Dutch oven over medium-high heat. Squeeze the sausage from the casing into the oil and brown, breaking up any clumps, about 3 minutes.

Gradually stir in the broth and 2 cups of water, and bring to a boil. Add the farro and red pepper flakes (if using). Cover and cook over medium heat until the farro is tender, 15 to 20 minutes.

Turn the farro and any unabsorbed liquid out of the pot into a serving bowl. Stir the sun-dried tomatoes into the farro.

Bring ½ cup of water to a boil in the pot. Add half the escarole. Cover and cook over medium-high heat until it wilts, about 1 minute, and then add the remaining escarole. Cover and cook until the escarole is tender, 3 to 5 minutes.

Stir the farro back into the pot and simmer for a few minutes to meld the flavors. Season with the lemon zest, and salt and pepper to taste.

OTHER IDEAS

• Substitute Swiss chard for the escarole.

• Vegetarian version: Omit the sausage. Omit the water and chicken broth, and use 1 quart vegetable broth. After cooking, stir in ½ cup toasted, chopped hazelnuts and 1 to 2 teaspoons chopped fresh rosemary. Serve with a bowl of grated Parmesan cheese.

lamb with millet and mint-cucumber salad

For a fresh finish, accompany this millet-lamb pilaf with thinly sliced cucumbers doused in yogurt and flecked with mint—dinner and a side salad all on one plate.

SERVES 4

For the millet

1 cup millet

1 tablespoon olive oil

1 cup chopped onion

¾ teaspoon ground cinnamon

¼ teaspoon ground allspice

12 ounces ground lamb

1 teaspoon salt

Freshly ground black pepper

For the mint-cucumber salad

3 cups thinly sliced, seeded cucumbers
   (2 medium)

1 cup low-fat plain yogurt

⅓ cup chopped fresh mint

¼ teaspoon ground cumin

½ teaspoon harissa, or to taste (optional)

1 teaspoon salt

Freshly ground black pepper

Set a heavy 3-quart Dutch oven over medium-high heat. Add the millet and toast, stirring frequently until aromatic, about 3 minutes.

Stir in the olive oil, onion, cinnamon, and allspice. Cook for 1 minute. Stir in the lamb. (It's fine that the lamb will get coated with the millet.) Keep stirring and breaking up the lamb for 1 minute. Cover and continue cooking until the lamb loses its pink color, 1 or 2 minutes longer.

Stir in 2¼ cups of water and the salt. Cover and simmer over low heat until most or all of the water has been absorbed, and the millet is tender, 15 to 20 minutes. Turn off the heat and let stand for 5 to 10 minutes, or until ready to serve.

Meanwhile, make the mint-cucumber salad: In a bowl, combine the cucumber, yogurt, ¼ cup of the mint, cumin, harissa (if using), and salt and pepper.

To serve, create a mound of the millet mixture on each plate. Surround with a generous amount of the mint-cucumber salad. Garnish with the remaining mint.

millet with collards and ham

Millet's mild flavor makes it a good foil for the assertive taste of collards and chunks of salty ham. Many cooks avoid collards because they think that these hearty, calcium-packed greens require long cooking. On the contrary, quickly sautéed, sprightly green collards are quite tender.

When shopping for collards, look for firm verdant leaves. If you see limp, yellowed bunches, pass them by. Be forewarned: like all hearty greens, collards shrink to about 20 percent of their original volume as they cook.

SERVES 4 TO 6

1 bunch collards (about 1½ pounds)

1 cup millet

2 tablespoons olive oil

1 tablespoon minced dried onion

2 teaspoons Cajun seasoning mix

½ teaspoon granulated garlic

3 cups low-sodium chicken or vegetable broth, plus more if needed

8 to 12 ounces ham steak, cut into ½-inch cubes

1½ cups frozen corn kernels

1 cup diced roasted red bell pepper, preferably fire-roasted

1 tablespoon mustard, preferably whole grain

Salt and freshly ground black pepper

SPEED TIP: Use a 1-pound bag of frozen collards to reduce prep time. Run them under hot water to partially thaw before adding to the pot.

Hold half the collards in a bunch. Cut off and discard all but about 2 inches of the stems. Thinly slice the remaining stems. Repeat with remaining collards. Set the stems aside. Stack the leaves. Cut lengthwise in half along the rib. Roll into a long cylinder and cut crosswise into ½-inch slivers. Rinse well in a large bowl of water. Place in a large colander and set aside.

Set a heavy 6-quart Dutch oven over medium-high heat. Add the millet and toast, stirring frequently until aromatic, about 3 minutes.

Push the millet to one side. Pour the olive oil onto an empty spot and stir in the onion, Cajun seasoning, and garlic. Cook for 10 seconds while stirring; stir in the millet.

Gradually stir in the broth and ham. Bring to a boil. Cover and boil over medium heat for 18 minutes. If there is no unabsorbed liquid, stir in ½ cup water or additional broth.

Place the collards on top of the millet. (If they don't all fit, cover and cook until the first batch wilts, about 1 minute; then set the remaining collards on top.) Don't stir the collards into the millet at this point; the millet cooks more evenly in liquid than in steam.

OTHER IDEAS

• **Substitute kale for the collards.**

Millet Casserole: Spoon the cooked mixture into a baking dish. Sprinkle on enough grated Cheddar or Monterey Jack cheese to cover the top. Set in the microwave or under a hot broiler until the cheese is melted. (This is a tasty way to recycle leftovers.)

Cover and continue cooking until the millet and collards are tender and most or all of the liquid has been absorbed, 5 to 7 minutes longer. If the mixture gets dry before the millet or collards are tender, add a bit more water or broth and cook over low heat for a few more minutes.

When the millet is tender (it usually cooks unevenly, leaving some grains a little firmer than others), stir in the corn, roasted bell pepper, and mustard. Add salt and black pepper to taste. Turn off the heat, cover, and let sit for 5 minutes or until ready to serve.

quinoa paella with chicken and chorizo

I'm sure that a traditional Spanish cook would find it odd to make a paella based on quinoa, but the concept works well. More important, it tastes good.

SERVES 4

1 pound boneless chicken thighs or breasts, cut into 1-inch pieces

Salt and freshly ground black pepper

1 tablespoon olive oil

1 teaspoon smoked Spanish paprika or other paprika

½ teaspoon granulated garlic

¼ to ½ teaspoon crushed red pepper flakes, to taste

3½ cups low-sodium chicken broth, plus more if needed

1 tablespoon tomato paste

2 cups quinoa

½ cup finely chopped dry-cured chorizo

1 cup frozen peas

½ cup thin strips roasted red bell pepper, preferably fire-roasted

3 tablespoons chopped fresh flat-leaf parsley

Season the chicken with salt and pepper. In a heavy 3-quart Dutch oven, heat the oil over high heat. Brown the chicken pieces, using tongs to turn, about 2 minutes on each side. Transfer the chicken to a plate.

Turn off the heat and let the pan cool for a minute. Stir the paprika, garlic, and red pepper flakes into the hot oil in the pot.

Stir the broth into the pot, taking care to scrape up any browned bits sticking to the bottom. Blend in the tomato paste, and bring to a boil over high heat. Stir in the quinoa and chorizo. Cover and reduce the heat to medium. Cook for 12 minutes.

Add salt to taste. Stir in the chicken. Cover and cook over low heat until the quinoa is done—it should have no opaque white dot in the center—and the chicken is cooked through, 2 to 3 minutes. If the mixture seems dry and the chicken or quinoa is not thoroughly cooked, stir in a little more broth or some water, cover, and cook a few minutes longer.

Stir in the peas and roasted red pepper. Cover and let sit for 1 minute. Stir in the parsley just before serving.

OTHER IDEAS

• Use cooked chicken or turkey; skip the browning step and simply stir it in for the last few minutes of cooking.
• Add 6 ounces peeled, medium shrimp; stir them in for the last few minutes of cooking.

coconut chicken curry with thai black rice

Thai black rice (also called Thai black sticky rice) is slightly sweet and traditionally steamed and used in desserts. Nevertheless, it makes a very tasty savory base for a savory curry, and its distinctive color makes the dish really striking.

SERVES 4

2 cups Thai black sticky rice, rinsed

¼ teaspoon salt

1 can (14 ounces) unsweetened coconut milk

½ tablespoon Thai red or green curry paste, plus more to taste

1¼ teaspoons Thai fish sauce

⅛ teaspoon granulated garlic

2 scallions, thinly sliced (keep white and green parts separate)

1 small red bell pepper, seeded and thinly sliced

1⅓ cups frozen shelled edamame

1¼ pounds boneless chicken breasts or thighs, cut into 1-inch chunks

20 to 25 large basil leaves

Japanese soy sauce (tamari or shoyu), to taste (optional)

Make the rice: In a heavy 2-quart Dutch oven, bring 3½ cups of water to a rapid boil. Add the rice and salt and return to a boil. Cover, reduce the heat, and simmer until the rice is tender, 25 to 30 minutes. Drain off any unabsorbed water. Return the rice to the pot and let steam, covered, until ready to use.

When the rice is just about done, prepare the curry: Combine the coconut milk, curry paste, fish sauce, and garlic in a heavy 3-quart Dutch oven. Add the scallion whites, bell pepper, and edamame. Bring to a gentle boil and cook for 2 minutes.

Stir in the chicken. Cover and simmer until the chicken and edamame are cooked, 3 to 5 minutes. Turn off the heat. Tear the basil leaves and stir them in. Season with soy sauce, if needed.

To serve, spoon the black rice into the center of large, shallow bowls. Ladle the curry around the rice. Garnish with the scallion greens.

OTHER IDEAS

• Use shrimp instead of chicken. Add the shrimp when the edamame are close to tender.

• Substitute ½ cup chopped cilantro for the basil.

• Use Minute brown rice instead of black. Follow the directions from the first paragraph of procedures on page 116, then add 1¾ cups water, cover, and cook over medium heat for 5 minutes, then let sit off the heat for 5 minutes.

curried brown rice with smoked trout

This unusual pilaf was inspired by the English dish called kedgeree. *When English colonials lived in India, they developed kedgeree as a way of combining their beloved kippers with their newfound enthusiasm for curry. Of course, they used white rice, but brown rice stands up even better to the intense flavor of the fish.*

Since it's not easy to find kippered herring in the United States, I've suggested smoked trout.

This is a terrific dish for a light supper. Avoid any temptation to omit the hard-boiled eggs; they add delicious balance to the salty fish.

SERVES 4

2 cups Minute brown rice

1 tablespoon butter

2 teaspoons minced dried onion

2 teaspoons mild Madras curry powder

10 to 12 ounces smoked trout, flaked, large
   bones discarded

1 cup frozen peas

3 hard-boiled large eggs, peeled and coarsely
   chopped

3 tablespoons chopped fresh parsley

Salt and freshly ground black pepper

Lemon wedges and mango chutney, for serving

Set a heavy 3-quart Dutch oven over medium-high heat. Add the rice and toast until aromatic, stirring frequently, about 3 minutes.

Reduce the heat to medium. Push the rice aside and place the butter on the empty side of the pot. As the butter melts, stir in the onion and curry powder and heat for about 10 seconds while stirring.

Gradually add 1¾ cups of water and the flaked fish. Cover and cook over medium heat for 5 minutes.

Stir in the peas. Turn off the heat. Cover and let sit for 5 minutes.

Mix in the eggs and parsley. Season to taste with salt and pepper. Serve with lemon wedges and a bowl of chutney.

OTHER IDEAS
- Add ½ teaspoon whole cumin seeds or ¼ teaspoon ground along with the curry powder.
- Substitute smoked mackerel or chopped, trimmed smoked salmon for the trout.

chili brown rice with chicken, black beans, and olives

This chili-scented, salsa-seasoned pilaf is based on brown rice and cooked chicken and is good right out of the pot or at room temperature.

Since avocado goes extremely well with brown rice, tomatoes, and black beans, I hope you can find a nice ripe specimen when you decide to prepare this pilaf. I've given a wide range of chili powder since individual blends vary so much in flavor and heat.

SERVES 4 TO 6

3 cups Minute brown rice

1 tablespoon olive oil

2 teaspoons to 2 tablespoons chili powder
   (depending upon taste and brand)

½ teaspoon ground cumin

½ teaspoon dried oregano

1 cup chunky salsa, plus more to taste and for
   serving

Salt

1 can (15 ounces) black beans, drained and rinsed

1 cup frozen corn

3 cups diced cooked chicken

½ cup pitted black olives, halved if large

1 ripe, firm Hass avocado, diced

⅓ cup pumpkin seeds, toasted

¼ cup chopped fresh cilantro

2 to 3 tablespoons freshly squeezed lime juice,
   to taste

Freshly ground black pepper

Sour cream, grated Cheddar or pepper Jack cheese,
   chopped red onion, for serving (optional)

Set a heavy 3-quart Dutch oven over medium heat. Add the rice and toast, stirring occasionally, until aromatic, 3 to 4 minutes.

Turn the heat to low. Push the rice aside and spoon the olive oil onto the empty spot in the pot. Stir in 2 teaspoons (or more if you are familiar with your brand) chili powder, the cumin, and oregano, and toast for 15 seconds.

Gradually stir in 2½ cups of water. Then stir in the salsa and ½ teaspoon salt. Taste the liquid. Stir in additional chili powder, if needed.

Bring to a boil over high heat. Cover and reduce the heat so that the liquid simmers. Cook for 5 minutes. If the rice isn't close to tender and all of the liquid has been absorbed, add ¼ to ½ cup hot water.

Stir in the beans, corn, chicken, and olives. If the mixture seems dry, stir in a bit more salsa. Cover and continue cooking for 1 more minute. Turn off the heat and let sit, covered, for 4 minutes.

Stir in the avocado, pumpkin seeds, and cilantro. Add lime juice, salt, and pepper to taste. Serve with bowls of salsa, sour cream, cheese, and onion, if desired.

OTHER IDEAS

- Serve at room temperature on a bed of shredded lettuce.
- Wrap in a whole-grain tortilla or tuck into a pita with some shredded red cabbage for lunch.
- Bring up the heat and smokiness by stirring in 1 to 2 teaspoons mashed chipotle in adobo along with the salsa.
- Add strips of roasted red pepper when you add the corn.

dinners from the oven

Oat-flecked Meat Loaves

Anything Goes Pizza

Bean-Chorizo Tortilla Stack

Black Bean Enchiladas

Tortilla Lasagne

Goat Cheese and Corn Enchiladas

Torticotti

oat-flecked meat loaves

Adding oatmeal to meat loaf probably started as a way to stretch the meat, but I've come to love the silken texture it provides.

Making the loaves free-form rather than using a loaf pan has four advantages: they cook more quickly, you can add as many goodies as you like, there's no pan to clean, and any fat drains away.

Each loaf serves 4, so you can freeze one or have plenty of extra to make sandwiches the next day. For those who agree with my volunteer recipe tester, Rita Yaezel, that meat loaf looks naked without gravy, try my quick version of her recipe in Other Ideas below.

MAKES 2 LOAVES; SERVES 8

1 cup oatmeal (old-fashioned rolled oats)

½ cup whole milk

2 large eggs

1 medium onion, finely chopped

1 cup chopped roasted red bell pepper, preferably fire-roasted

½ cup ketchup

¼ cup chopped fresh parsley

1½ teaspoons dried Italian seasoning blend

¾ teaspoon granulated garlic

1 teaspoon salt

2 to 2¼ pounds meat loaf mix, or about 12 ounces each ground veal, beef, and pork

1 small green bell pepper, seeded and cut into thin strips

OTHER IDEAS

• Add one or more of the following to the meat loaf mixture: ½ cup chopped pimento-stuffed green olives, 1 cup frozen corn kernels, 3 tablespoons chopped capers, ⅓ cup chopped sun-dried tomatoes packed in oil, ½ to 1 teaspoon crushed red pepper flakes, 1 teaspoon Japanese soy sauce (shoyu or tamari).

• Use a smoky barbecue sauce instead of ketchup.

• Make 1 meat loaf and shape the rest of the mixture into burgers and freeze. Defrost as needed and pan-fry.

• Make a quick gravy by sautéing 8 ounces sliced mushrooms and a small, chopped onion in olive oil over medium-high heat, stirring frequently, for 3 minutes. Stir in 2 tablespoons tomato paste, ¼ teaspoon each dried thyme and oregano, and ⅛ teaspoon salt, and continue cooking and stirring for 1 minute more. Stir in 3 tablespoons whole-wheat pastry flour. Add 3 cups low-sodium chicken broth. Bring to a gentle boil, stirring all the while to avoid lumping. Continue cooking over medium heat, stirring frequently, until the gravy thickens and the flour tastes cooked, about 5 minutes. Adjust seasonings with salt and pepper to taste. Makes about 3 cups.

> **SPEED TIP:** Pulse the onion, roasted red pepper, and parsley together in the food processor until finely chopped. Don't run the motor at full speed, which will turn them to mush.

Place a rack in the center of the oven and preheat the oven to 375°F. Line the bottom of a broiler pan with foil for easy cleanup and set the top perforated dripping pan in place.

In a small bowl, combine the oats and milk. Stir occasionally to coax the oatmeal into absorbing the milk.

Meanwhile, lightly beat the eggs in a large bowl. Stir in the onion, roasted red pepper, ketchup, parsley, Italian seasonings, garlic, and salt. Add the ground meat and the oats with any unabsorbed milk. Blend well with your hands.

Divide the mixture in half and shape into two rectangular or square loaves about 3 inches thick. Place them on the broiler pan. Arrange the strips of green bell pepper decoratively on top of each loaf and gently press them into place. Bake for 15 minutes. Rotate the pan. Continue baking until the loaves feel firm to the touch, and an instant thermometer inserted into the center reads 160°F, 20 to 25 minutes longer. If you'd like to brown the tops, set the loaves under the broiler.

Let the loaves rest for 5 to 10 minutes before slicing. Once cool, the meat loaves can be refrigerated for up to 5 days or frozen for up to 2 months.

anything goes pizza

Trader Joe's calls its prebaked whole-wheat pizza crust "tabula rasa," the perfect name because the crust is truly a blank slate on which you can arrange whatever ingredients you have on hand.

The ingredients and amounts below are just suggestions to get your imagination rolling. For a Greek pizza, use feta cheese, zucchini, and Kalamata olives. For a Mediterranean pizza, use white beans and goat cheese. For more international topping ideas, see the chart on page 123.

SERVES 3 TO 4

1 prepared whole-wheat pizza crust (1 pound), about 14 inches diameter

2 teaspoons olive oil

1 cup pasta sauce

1½ tablespoons pesto

2 cups shredded smoked mozzarella

½ cup black oil-cured olives

½ cup thinly sliced salami

1 cup sliced baby portobellos

¼ cup grated Parmesan cheese

Set a rack in the middle of the oven and preheat the oven to 425°F.

Set the pizza crust on a large baking pan. Brush the olive oil around the edges of the crust to encourage crisping.

Combine the pasta sauce and pesto and spread it on top. Distribute the mozzarella, olives, salami, and mushrooms over the sauce. Sprinkle on the Parmesan cheese.

Bake until the cheese is melted and the edges are crisp, 8 to 12 minutes. Let rest for a few minutes before slicing.

OTHER IDEAS

• Try some fully cooked sliced chicken or turkey sausages instead of salami. Add it a few minutes before the pizza is done.

• Add some cooked chopped broccoli or zucchini for the final few minutes of cooking.

• Make individual pizzas on whole-wheat pitas or lavash.

• Sprinkle on chopped fresh rosemary or oregano just before serving.

Pizza Toppings

Use this chart as a jumping-off point to travel from one culinary country to the next by changing toppings. Use one or a combination of items from each column. Mix dried herbs into the sauce. Sprinkle on fresh herbs after heating in the microwave or an oven set to 375°.

THEME	SAUCE	CHEESE	HERBS	OTHER OPTIONS
ITALIAN	tomato pesto tapenade	mozzarella grated Parmesan grated Romano provolone	basil parsley	anchovies salami prosciutto capers black olives
TEX-MEX	salsa	Monterey pepper Jack, queso fresco	cilantro	corn kernels chorizo black beans sliced red onion pimento-stuffed olives
GREEK	tomato	feta	parsley, oregano	kalamata olives, roasted red peppers, halved cherry tomatoes
MOROCCAN	tomato mixed with a little harissa	feta	mint	chopped cooked lamb, chickpeas, roasted red peppers

bean-chorizo tortilla stack

Use readily available whole-grain tortillas to assemble a fetching layered casserole that combines the ingredients of Mexican and Spanish kitchens. For advice on selecting tortillas, see page 28.

SERVES 4

1 teaspoon olive oil

4 whole-grain tortillas, about 10 inches in diameter

1 can (15 ounces) black beans, drained and rinsed

½ cup finely chopped dry-cured chorizo

½ cup pimento-stuffed olives, coarsely chopped

1½ cups frozen corn

1½ cups shredded Monterey pepper Jack cheese

1½ cups chunky salsa

1 tablespoon chopped fresh cilantro

Set rack in the middle of the oven, and preheat the oven to 400°F. Brush the oil on the bottom and sides of a 10-inch pie plate or equivalent covered ovenproof baking dish.

If one tortilla is larger than the others, set it aside to use on the top. Set 2 tortillas in the bottom of the pie plate. Distribute half the beans, chorizo, olives, and corn, and ½ cup of the cheese on the tortilla. Drop ½ cup of the salsa in spoonfuls on top.

Set a tortilla over the mixture, and make a second layer with the remaining beans, chorizo, olives, and corn. Distribute ½ cup cheese and salsa on top.

Set the last, largest tortilla in place. Spread the remaining ½ cup salsa on top. Spray or brush a piece of foil lightly with oil to prevent sticking. Cover the pie plate tightly with foil.

Bake for 15 minutes. Remove the foil. Sprinkle the remaining ½ cup cheese over the salsa. Continue baking until the cheese is melted and the casserole is heated through to the center, 10 to 20 minutes longer.

Sprinkle the cilantro on top. Let rest for 5 minutes before cutting into quarters. Use a spatula to transfer onto plates.

OTHER IDEAS
- Serve with a dollop of sour cream on top of each portion.
- Instead of dry-cured chorizo, use fully cooked chorizo sausage. Increase the amount to 1 cup.
- Use ripe black olives instead of green.

black bean enchiladas

It's easy to switch from tortillas made of refined flour to those made of whole wheat, and it's unlikely that anyone will even notice the difference. Prior to working on this book, I used tortillas only to make sandwich-style wraps, never realizing how easy it is to make enchiladas.

Granted, my idea of an enchilada would probably make even the most easygoing Mexican cook blanch. I haven't aimed for authenticity here, just convenience and good taste.

The trickiest thing about enchiladas is figuring out how many each one will serve. One is usually enough for me, one and a half is just right for many people, and big eaters require two. This recipe can easily be doubled, and extras freeze well.

MAKES 4 ENCHILADAS; SERVES 2 TO 4

1 ripe, firm Hass avocado, diced

2 tablespoons freshly squeezed lime juice

Salt

1 can (15 ounce) black beans, drained and rinsed

½ cup diced roasted red bell pepper, preferably
  fire-roasted

1 cup shredded sharp Cheddar cheese

½ cup frozen corn

⅓ cup finely chopped red onion

¼ cup chopped fresh cilantro

1¼ cups chunky salsa, preferably fire-roasted,
  plus more to pass at the table

4 large whole-wheat tortillas, about 10 inches
  in diameter

Shredded romaine lettuce and lime wedges, for
  serving

Toss the avocado in lime juice and sprinkle lightly with salt. Set aside.

To make the filling, in a medium bowl, combine the beans, roasted red pepper, ½ cup of the cheese, corn, onion, cilantro, and ¼ cup of the salsa. Add salt to taste.

Distribute ½ cup of filling across the middle of each tortilla. Roll up. Set 2 enchiladas, seam side down, on a microwavable dinner plate. Pour a strip of salsa along the length of each tortilla. Sprinkle with cheese. Repeat to make 2 more enchiladas. Cover lightly with waxed paper to catch splatters. Microwave until heated throughout, about 3 minutes for both of them together.

Alternatively, before sprinkling on the cheese, heat the enchiladas on a nonstick pan, in an oven preheated to 375°F for 15 minutes. Sprinkle on the cheese and continue heating until the cheese is melted and bubbly and the enchiladas are piping hot.

To serve, tuck some shredded lettuce under and around the enchiladas. Set some diced avocado to one side and a lime wedge to the other side. Accompany the enchiladas with a bowl of the remaining cup of salsa.

OTHER IDEAS
• Add ¼ to ½ teaspoon of ground, dried chipotle to the filling.
• Use jalapeño Jack instead of Cheddar cheese.
• Use enchilada sauce instead of salsa, but read the label first, to make sure there isn't too much sugar or corn syrup: many enchilada sauces are very sweet.

tortilla lasagne

Large store-bought tortillas make a quick and easy alternative to traditional lasagne noodles in this layered casserole. Now that so many "flavors" and colors of tortillas and burrito wraps are readily available, it's great to keep them on hand in the freezer for last-minute creations like this one.

Rather than using a rectangular baking pan, I follow the shape of the tortilla by baking the layered dish in a pie plate. Because the plate is fairly shallow, it heats up quickly—usually in less than a half hour.

Serve the "lasagne" with a salad of arugula and chopped fennel tossed with a lemony vinaigrette.

SERVES 4

1 teaspoon olive oil

1 jar (24 to 28 ounces) pasta sauce with mushrooms

1 package (10 ounces) frozen chopped spinach, defrosted

1 cup reduced-fat ricotta

⅓ cup pitted, oil-cured black olives, coarsely chopped

5 to 6 whole-wheat tortillas, about 10 inches in diameter

2 ounces sliced salami, quartered (½ cup)

7 ounces loosely packed shredded mozzarella cheese (1½ cups)

3 tablespoons grated Parmesan cheese, plus more to pass at the table

OTHER IDEAS
• Stir some pesto or black olive tapenade into the pasta sauce.
• Add ½ to 1 teaspoon crushed red pepper flakes to the pasta sauce.
• Use chopped prosciutto or speck instead of salami.
• Omit the salami and use a pasta sauce that contains sausage.
• Used smoked mozzarella instead of plain.
• Spread a generous amount of chopped fresh basil on each layer.

Set a rack in the middle of the oven, and preheat the oven to 400°F. Brush the oil on the bottom and sides of a 10-inch pie plate or equivalent covered ovenproof baking dish.

Pour the sauce into a medium bowl. Squeeze the spinach to discard excess liquid. Blend the spinach, ricotta, and all but 2 tablespoons of the olives into the sauce.

If one tortilla is larger than the others, set it aside. Set 2 tortillas on the pie plate, overlapping if necessary, to cover the bottom. Distribute one-third of the sauce mixture on top. Scatter on half the salami and ½ cup of the mozzarella. Set a tortilla on top.

Make a second layer with another third of the sauce mixture, the remaining salami, and ½ cup of the cheese.

Set the last, largest tortilla on top. Spread the remaining sauce, ½ cup cheese, and 2 tablespoons olives on top.

Brush or spray a sheet of foil lightly with oil to prevent sticking. Cover the pie plate with the foil, securing tightly around the sides, leaving a little airspace on top. Set the plate on a cookie sheet to catch any bubble-overs.

Bake for 20 minutes. Remove the foil, rotate the pan, and continue baking until the casserole is heated through to the center and the liquid is bubbling, 5 to 10 minutes longer.

Set on a rack. Sprinkle the top with Parmesan cheese and let rest for 5 minutes. Cut into quarters and use a spatula to transfer onto plates. Accompany with a small bowl of Parmesan.

goat cheese and corn enchiladas

This unusual take on enchiladas is elegant enough to serve to company. Because the filling is rich, one enchilada per person should be just right. Double or triple the recipe, as your needs require.

Serve the enchiladas with a large tossed green salad dressed with a lime juice–olive oil vinaigrette.

MAKES 2 ENCHILADAS; SERVES 1 TO 2

3½ to 4 ounces fresh goat cheese (about ½ cup tightly packed), at room temperature

1 tablespoon brine from jarred roasted red peppers

½ teaspoon ground cumin

½ teaspoon smoked Spanish paprika or other paprika

½ cup frozen corn

⅓ cup chopped roasted red pepper, preferably fire-roasted

3 tablespoons chopped fresh cilantro, plus more for serving

1 scallion (white and green parts), thinly sliced

2 whole-wheat tortillas, about 10 inches in diameter

½ cup chunky salsa

To make the filling, in a medium bowl, blend the goat cheese, brine, cumin, and paprika. Stir in the corn, roasted red pepper, cilantro, and scallion.

Distribute ½ cup of filling across the middle of each tortilla. Roll up. Set the 2 enchiladas, seam side down, on a microwavable dinner plate. Pour a strip of salsa along the length of each tortilla. Cover lightly with waxed paper to catch splatters. Microwave until heated throughout, about 3 minutes.

Alternatively, heat the enchiladas on a nonstick baking pan, in an oven preheated to 375°F, until heated throughout, 15 to 20 minutes.

Garnish with cilantro and serve immediately.

OTHER IDEAS

• For a heartier filling, add some diced cooked chicken or black beans.

torticotti

This easy variation on the theme of manicotti calls for whole-wheat tortillas wrapped around a ricotta filling. Having the tortillas ready to go obviates the need to precook pasta as a separate step. Practicality aside, it's just darn good.

Figure that an average eater will have one and a big eater either one and a half or two. Serve the torticotti with fried peppers and onions or a tricolored salad of radicchio, arugula, and endive.

MAKES 4; SERVES 2 TO 4

1 package (10 ounces) frozen spinach, defrosted

2 cups reduced-fat ricotta cheese

3 tablespoons store-bought pesto

¼ cup grated Romano cheese, plus more for serving

2 tablespoons balsamic vinegar

1 teaspoon salt

¼ teaspoon granulated garlic

½ cup toasted, chopped hazelnuts or walnuts

4 whole-wheat tortillas, about 10 inches in diameter

1 cup pasta sauce, preferably with mushrooms

Squeeze the excess liquid from the spinach. Place the spinach, ricotta, pesto, Romano cheese, vinegar, salt, and garlic in a food processor. (Alternatively, blend them together by hand.) Stir in the hazelnuts.

Spread ¾ cup of filling down the center of each tortilla. Fold each side over to cover the filling. Set 2 torticotti, seam side down, on a large microwaveable plate. Spread about ¼ cup of sauce on top of each. Repeat to make 2 more torticotti. Cover lightly with waxed paper to catch splatters.

Microwave until heated throughout, about 3 minutes for two and 5 minutes for four.

Alternatively, heat the torticotti, lightly tented with foil, on a nonstick baking pan, in an oven preheated to 375°F, until piping hot, 15 to 20 minutes.

Garnish with Romano cheese before serving.

OTHER IDEAS
- **Add ½ teaspoon crushed red pepper flakes to the filling.**
- **Scatter shredded mozzarella (smoked is especially nice) on top of the pasta sauce.**
- **After heating, garnish with a little chopped fresh parsley.**

main-dish grain salads

Dilled Barley and Chicken Salad

Bulgur Salad with Tuna, Olives, and Feta

Aztec Couscous Salad

Couscous Chicken Salad with Double-Citrus Dressing

Farro Salad with Chickpeas and Marinated Artichoke Hearts

Brown Rice, Baked Tofu, and Asian Slaw with Soy-Lime Vinaigrette

Beet Salad with Chicken, Orzo, and Kumquats

Fruity-Nutty Wild Rice and Turkey Salad

dilled barley and chicken salad

Mild-mannered, gently chewy barley makes an appealing base for a grain salad, especially for newcomers to whole grains. This colorful, refreshing mix is made with ingredients familiar to everyone and easily kept on hand. It's great to bring to a potluck.

SERVES 4

1 cup quick-cooking barley

½ teaspoon salt, plus more to taste

2 cups chopped cooked chicken

1½ cups grated carrot

½ cup walnut halves, toasted

¼ cup dried currants

½ cup (tightly packed) chopped fresh dill

¼ cup olive oil

3 to 4 tablespoons freshly squeezed lemon
    juice, to taste

In a heavy 2-quart Dutch oven, bring 2¼ cups of water to a rapid boil. Stir in the barley and ¼ teaspoon salt.

Cover and cook over medium heat until the barley is tender, about 10 minutes. Drain off any excess water. Spread on a plate to cool.

In a large bowl, combine the chicken, carrot, walnuts, and currants. Add the barley and dill.

Toss in the oil, 3 tablespoons lemon juice, and ¼ teaspoon salt. Add more salt and lemon juice, if needed.

OTHER IDEAS
- **Used cooked brown rice or quinoa instead of barley.**
- **Try sherry wine vinegar instead of lemon juice.**

bulgur salad with tuna, olives, and feta

Bulgur and tuna both stand up well to the assertive flavors of a Greek salad, including feta, oregano, and Kalamata olives.

Serve the salad on a bed of soft butter lettuce with some warm whole-wheat pita and hummus on the side.

SERVES 4

---

3 tablespoons olive oil

½ teaspoon dried oregano

¾ teaspoon salt, plus more to taste

1¼ cups coarse bulgur

6 ounces feta cheese

1 can (6 ounces) tuna packed in olive oil

2½ cups diced, seeded cucumbers, preferably Kirby

½ cup pitted Kalamata olives, halved

Grated zest of 1 lemon

¼ cup freshly squeezed lemon juice, plus more to taste

Freshly ground black pepper

Pour the olive oil into a small bowl. Crumble in the oregano and stir. Set aside.

In a heavy 2-quart Dutch oven, bring 3 cups of water and the salt to a boil. Add the bulgur. Stir once and then cover and simmer until the grains are tender, about 20 minutes. Drain. Run under cold water to cool. Drain well.

Crumble the feta with your fingers into a salad bowl. Add the tuna (including oil), cucumbers, olives, and bulgur.

Toss in the oregano-olive oil, lemon zest, and juice. Season to taste with salt and pepper and extra lemon juice, if needed.

OTHER IDEAS
- **Add 1 cup cherry tomatoes, halved.**
- **Toss in ¼ cup chopped fresh mint.**

aztec couscous salad

Because couscous is ready in about 5 minutes, it is probably the busy cook's best friend when it's time to get a meal together in a hurry. Here it acts as the base for a colorful salad based on many ingredients of the New World: chile peppers, corn, and beans.

It's a good salad to make when it feels too hot to cook and taste buds need a wake-up call.

SERVES 4 TO 6

1 cup frozen corn

1 cup whole-wheat couscous

3 tablespoons olive oil

½ teaspoon salt, plus more to taste

½ teaspoon ground cumin

⅛ teaspoon granulated garlic

1 can (15 ounces) black beans, drained and
   rinsed

2 scallions (white and green parts), thinly sliced

⅓ cup (tightly packed) chopped fresh cilantro

⅓ cup diced roasted red bell pepper, preferably
   fire-roasted

1 large jalapeño pepper, seeded and finely
   chopped

3 to 4 tablespoons freshly squeezed lime juice,
   to taste

Bring about 3 cups of water to a boil in a kettle. Place the corn in a strainer and run about half the boiling water over it to defrost. Drain well.

Place the couscous in a heavy 2-quart Dutch oven. Use a wooden spoon to vigorously stir in 1 tablespoon of the olive oil. Continue stirring until the little beads of couscous are thoroughly coated with the oil. Add the salt, cumin, garlic, and corn.

Stir 1 to 1½ cups boiling water (according to couscous package instructions) into the couscous. Cover and let sit off heat for 5 minutes. Fluff up with a fork.

While the couscous is steeping, combine the beans, scallions, cilantro, roasted red pepper, and jalapeño in a large bowl. Toss in the couscous mixture, the remaining 2 tablespoons olive oil, and the lime juice. Season with additional salt, if needed.

OTHER IDEAS

• **Use 2 to 4 tablespoons chopped, pickled jalapeño instead of fresh.**
• **Add ¼ cup chopped pimento-stuffed olives.**
• **Stuff the salad into whole-wheat pita with some shredded lettuce or chopped watercress.**
• **Use the couscous salad to stuff scooped-out beefsteak tomatoes or halved avocadoes.**

couscous chicken salad with double-citrus dressing

This unusual salad was created by Sukran Demirel, one of the most imaginative cooks I know. The carrot ribbons—made simply with a potato peeler—make the dish very festive. Including both lemon and lime juices and zests in the dressing tastes doubly snappy.

SERVES 2 TO 3

For the salad

1 cup whole-wheat couscous

1 tablespoon olive oil

¼ teaspoon salt, plus more to taste

1 large carrot, trimmed and peeled

1 unpeeled Granny Smith apple, cored and diced

2 to 3 cups chopped, cooked chicken

½ cup slivered almonds, toasted

¼ cup chopped fresh cilantro

For the dressing

¼ cup olive oil

Grated zest of 1 lemon

Grated zest of 1 lime

3 tablespoons freshly squeezed lemon juice

2 tablespoons freshly squeezed lime juice

1 teaspoon Japanese soy sauce (shoyu or tamari)

½ teaspoon salt, plus more to taste

Mesclun, for serving

Bring about 2 cups of water to a boil in a kettle. Place the couscous in a heavy 2-quart Dutch oven. Use a fork to vigorously stir in the 1 tablespoon of olive oil. Continue stirring until the little beads of couscous are thoroughly coated with the oil.

Stir 1 to 1½ cups boiling water (according to package instructions) and the salt into the couscous. Cover and let sit off heat for 5 minutes. Fluff up with a fork.

While the couscous is steeping, use a vegetable peeler to peel the carrot into thin ribbons.

In a medium bowl, toss together the carrot ribbons, apple, chicken, almonds, and cilantro. Add the couscous.

In a small bowl combine the olive oil, lemon and lime zests and juices, the soy sauce and salt. Toss the dressing into the salad. Add more salt, if needed.

Serve the salad on a bed of mesclun.

OTHER IDEAS

- Try shelled, roasted pistachios instead of almonds.
- Add ¼ cup dried currants or ⅓ cup dried cranberries.
- Add 1 cup thinly sliced endive.
- Substitute raw parsnip for the carrot.
- Add pomegranate seeds when they are in season.
- Use orange zest and juice instead of lime.

farro salad with chickpeas and marinated artichoke hearts

It's ideal to use farro—an ancient Italian cousin of wheat—in a salad because unlike many other grains, it doesn't harden when refrigerated, so you can make the salad in advance and even serve it chilled, if you like.

Because the farro is semi-pearled (some of the bran has been rubbed off), it cooks in under a half hour. In this salad I've combined farro with other ingredients common to the Mediterranean kitchen.

SERVES 5 TO 6

For the salad

1 small red onion, halved crosswise and thinly sliced

1 tablespoon balsamic vinegar

⅛ teaspoon salt

1½ cups semi-pearled farro

1 jar (12 ounces) marinated artichoke hearts, drained and quartered

1 can (15 ounces) chickpeas, drained and rinsed

⅓ cup chopped sun-dried tomatoes packed in oil

For the dressing

3 tablespoons olive oil (or oil from the sun-dried tomatoes)

3 tablespoons grated Romano cheese

Grated zest of 1 large lemon

3 tablespoons freshly squeezed lemon juice, plus more to taste

¼ cup chopped fresh flat-leaf parsley

Salt and freshly ground black pepper

Place the onion in a small bowl and stir in the balsamic. Set aside.

Bring 2½ cups of water and the salt to a boil in a heavy 2-quart Dutch oven. Add the farro. Cover and cook over medium-low heat until the farro is tender, 20 to 25 minutes. Drain off any unabsorbed liquid.

Combine the artichoke hearts, chickpeas, and sun-dried tomatoes in a medium serving or storage bowl. Toss in the farro and the onions with any unabsorbed balsamic.

To make the dressing, in the bowl used for the onion, combine the olive oil, Romano cheese, lemon zest, lemon juice, and parsley. Toss the dressing into the salad. Add salt and pepper to taste, plus additional lemon juice, if needed.

OTHER IDEAS
- Add finely diced salami or soppressata.
- Toss in some shredded radicchio just before serving.

brown rice, baked tofu, and asian slaw with soy-lime vinaigrette

Here is a light and crunchy East-West fusion salad based on brown rice. The lime dressing makes it especially refreshing to serve in warm weather.

You'll find baked tofu in the refrigerated section of health-food stores and in some supermarkets. To keep the cabbage crisp, add the dressing just before serving.

SERVES 4

1 cup Minute brown rice

6 cups (tightly packed), shredded Napa cabbage

8 ounces baked tofu, preferably Asian-spiced, diced

1 medium red bell pepper, seeded and cut into thin strips

⅓ cup chopped roasted peanuts

¼ cup freshly squeezed lime juice

¼ cup olive oil

1½ tablespoons Japanese soy sauce (tamari or shoyu)

1 teaspoon Chinese or Dijon mustard

¼ to ½ teaspoon chile-garlic paste, to taste

1 ripe Hass avocado, sliced

Set a heavy 2-quart Dutch oven over medium heat. Add the rice and toast, stirring occasionally, until it becomes aromatic, about 3 minutes.

Gradually stir in ¾ cup of water. Cover and reduce the heat to simmer. Cook for 5 minutes. Stir well. Turn off the heat, cover, and let steep for 5 minutes.

Transfer the rice to a large bowl and stir to release steam and cool. Toss in the cabbage, tofu, bell pepper, and peanuts.

In a small bowl, combine the lime juice, olive oil, soy sauce, mustard, and chile-garlic paste. Pour the dressing over the salad and toss to coat. Add more soy sauce, if needed.

Divide among four plates. Fan out avocado slices on top or to one side.

OTHER IDEAS
• Use green cabbage, or a mixture of green and red, instead of Napa.
• Add 2 tablespoons toasted sesame seeds. Black sesame seeds are especially pretty in this salad.

beet salad with chicken, orzo, and kumquats

This striking, beet-red salad satisfies all of your cravings for tart, sweet, bitter, and sour. I've had bad luck planning to make the salad and then not finding kumquats anywhere, so I let inspiration strike when I spot a container for sale in the supermarket. Many of the kumquats sold in America are grown in Florida and available from around mid-November through mid-April.

Unless you are carefully watching your salt intake, select salted canned beets as they have better flavor. This salad, with its fruity orange-soy vinaigrette, makes a great addition to a buffet table or pot luck.

SERVES 6

Salt

1 small red onion, halved and thinly sliced

2 tablespoons sherry or other wine vinegar

14 fresh, ripe kumquats

2 cans (15 ounces each) salted, sliced beets, drained

2 cups diced, cooked chicken

6 ounces farro orzo or other whole-grain orzo

¼ cup orange juice concentrate

2 tablespoons olive oil

1½ tablespoons Japanese soy sauce (tamari or shoyu), plus more to taste

½ cup walnuts, toasted and coarsely chopped

Bring a large pot of salted water to a boil.

Meanwhile, set the onion slices in a small bowl and add the vinegar. Stir well. (Marinating the onion briefly in vinegar reduces their pungency.)

Halve the kumquats crosswise and remove the seeds. Chop the kumquats fairly finely and place them in a large salad bowl. Stack the sliced beets and cut them into long, thin strips. Add them to the bowl, and toss in the chicken.

When the water is boiling, add the orzo and cook according to package directions until just short of tender. Start checking for doneness a few minutes early to avoid overcooking.

Meanwhile, prepare the dressing: In a large bowl, whisk together the orange juice concentrate, olive oil, soy sauce, and 2 tablespoons of the pasta water.

When the pasta is done, drain it well and add it to the bowl. Add the onion and any unabsorbed vinegar. Toss in the dressing. Add more soy sauce, if needed.

Garnish the salad liberally with walnuts.

OTHER IDEAS
• **Use ¼ cup toasted pine nuts instead of walnuts.**

fruity-nutty wild rice and turkey salad

As you can see from the picture in the photo insert, this is quite a festive dish. Wild rice, dense in flavor and texture, makes an ideal foil for juicy, sweet chunks of apple and orange—and cooked turkey, of course.

SERVES 3 TO 4

1¼ cups instant wild rice

⅛ teaspoon salt, plus more to taste

2½ cups diced, cooked roast turkey

2 navel oranges, peeled, halved horizontally, and separated into segments

1 unpeeled Granny Smith apple, cored and diced

⅓ cup dried cranberries

½ cup hazelnuts, toasted and coarsely chopped

3 tablespoons mayonnaise

⅔ cup orange juice

Combine the rice, 1¼ cups of water and the salt in a heavy 2-quart Dutch oven. Bring to a boil over high heat. Cover and reduce the heat so that the water simmers. Cook for 5 minutes. Stir well. Turn off the heat and let sit for 5 minutes.

While the rice is cooking, combine the turkey, oranges, apple, cranberries, and hazelnuts in a serving bowl.

In a small bowl, blend the mayonnaise and orange juice.

When the rice is done, drain off any unabsorbed liquid and toss it into the salad. Stir in the dressing and add salt to taste, if needed.

OTHER IDEAS
• Use chicken or ham instead of turkey.
• Add 3 tablespoons chopped fresh dill, or 2 teaspoons chopped fresh tarragon, or ¼ cup chopped fresh cilantro.
• Substitute 2 chopped pears for the apple.

grains on the side

Barley Pilaf with Fennel, Pecans, and Cranberries

Winter Squash with Barley and Ginger

Buckwheat with Cheddar and Pickled Jalapeños

Curried Bulgur with Beets

Mashed Millet with Cauliflower and Carrots

> *Millet-Cauliflower Pancakes*

> *Millet Casserole with Cheese*

Smoked Paprika Oats with Peas

Quinoa-Creamed Spinach

Polenta-Style Quinoa

Parmesan Brown Rice

Rye Flakes with Buttermilk, Caraway, and Dill

Wild Rice with Mushrooms, Potatoes, and Squash

barley pilaf with fennel, pecans, and cranberries

Barley contains a kind of starch that feels rich and creamy on the tongue and makes this festive dish moist and reminiscent of a Thanksgiving stuffing. Needless to say, it goes well with roast chicken or turkey. Unlike a traditional stuffing that is oven-baked for an hour or more, this one cooks in about 10 minutes on top of the stove— thanks to the quick-cooking barley flakes.

SERVES 4

1/3 cup pecans, coarsely chopped

2 cups barley flakes

1 tablespoon unsalted butter

1/2 teaspoon fennel seeds, chopped

2 cups low-sodium chicken broth

1/4 cup dried cranberries, coarsely chopped

1/4 teaspoon salt, plus more to taste

Freshly ground black pepper

Set a heavy 2-quart Dutch oven over medium heat. Add the pecans and toast until fragrant, stirring occasionally, about 2 minutes. Tip the nuts out of the pot onto a chopping board.

Add the barley flakes to the pot and toast, stirring frequently, until the flakes are aromatic, about 2 minutes. Push the barley aside. Add the butter to the empty side of the pot, and as it melts, stir in the fennel seeds. Let them sizzle in the butter for 30 seconds or so. Then stir the butter into the flakes.

Stir in the broth, cranberries, and salt. Bring to a boil. Cover and reduce the heat to low. Simmer for 5 minutes. If the flakes aren't tender and all of the liquid has been absorbed, stir in a few tablespoons of water, cover, and continue cooking until done.

Chop the pecans coarsely and stir them into the barley. Add salt and pepper to taste.

OTHER IDEAS
• Use rolled oats, spelt, or Kamut flakes instead of barley flakes.
• Try dried cherries, raisins, or dried currants instead of cranberries.
• Press portions of the pilaf into a coffee cup or ramekin and unmold onto plates.

winter squash with barley and ginger

If you are drawn to the taste of fresh ginger, here is a lovely fat-free way to surround winter squash and quick-cooking barley with its piquant flavor.

My favorite winter squash is kabocha, also called Hokkaido pumpkin. Its skin is either orange or green with stripes, the latter variety looking much like acorn squash (which can be used as a substitute).

This dish makes an attractive side dish to serve with a holiday roast turkey or baked ham.

SERVES 6

2 to 2½ pounds winter squash, such as kabocha, acorn, or hubbard

One 3-inch-long chubby knob of ginger

2 teaspoons minced dried onion

¾ cup quick-cooking barley

Salt

Microwave the whole squash for 4 minutes on high. (This brief precooking will make it much easier to cut the squash.) Let it cool for a few minutes.

Meanwhile, peel the ginger and finely chop it. You should have 2 to 3 tablespoons.

Peel the squash. Halve and remove the seeds. Cut the squash into 2-inch chunks.

In a heavy 3-quart Dutch oven, bring 1¾ cups of water to a boil. Stir in half the ginger plus the onion and barley. Set the squash on top of the barley, scattering the remaining ginger between the layers. Sprinkle lightly with salt. Do not stir at this point.

Cover and cook over medium heat until the squash is almost tender, 10 to 12 minutes. Turn off the heat and let the mixture sit until the barley and squash are tender, 3 to 5 minutes more. Stir well to thicken the sauce with very soft bits of squash. Add more salt, if needed.

OTHER IDEAS

• Drizzle each portion with a little store-bought peanut sauce. San-J is a good brand.

• Turn this recipe into a main dish by stirring in diced roast chicken or turkey, or fully cooked chicken sausage after the 10-minute cooking time. If using sausage, choose one whose flavors are compatible with the squash and ginger.

buckwheat with cheddar and pickled jalapeños

I prefer to prepare this casserole with mild, untoasted buckwheat, but the flavors stand up well to the stronger taste of toasted buckwheat, better known as kasha.

Vegetarians will find this hearty dish a satisfying entrée. Others will enjoy it as a side with broiled pork chops or grilled sausages.

SERVES 6 TO 8

2 tablespoons unsalted butter

2 tablespoons minced dried onion

1 teaspoon dried oregano

1½ cups untoasted buckwheat or toasted buckwheat (kasha)

1 teaspoon salt

1½ cups (tightly packed) shredded Cheddar cheese (about 4 ounces)

3 to 4 tablespoons finely chopped pickled jalapeños

Freshly ground black pepper

Set the butter in a heavy 3-quart Dutch oven, and turn the heat to medium-high. As the butter melts, stir in the onion. Cook until the onion begins to brown, about 1 minute. Stir in the oregano and cook for another 10 seconds.

Stir in the buckwheat, and coat the grains with the butter. Gradually stir in 3½ cups of water and the salt.

Bring to a boil over high heat. Cover, lower the heat, and simmer until most or all the liquid has been absorbed and the grains are close to tender, 10 to 12 minutes. Stir in the cheese and pickled jalapeños. Turn off the heat, cover, and let sit for 5 minutes. Adjust the seasonings with salt and pepper before serving.

OTHER IDEAS
• Omit the dried oregano, and stir in fresh chopped sage to taste before serving.

curried bulgur with beets

Toasty brown bulgur is transformed to a dramatic scarlet, thanks to the gorgeous color of beets. I did not realize how good canned beets could taste until exploring quick options for this book.

I also had never thought of combining beets with curry until my assistant, Sukran Demeril, suggested it, and what a splendid idea. Canned beets and the brand of curry I recommend both contain salt, so don't add any extra until you taste the cooked dish.

Serve this gorgeous side dish as part of an Indian meal or with lamb chops, roast chicken, or pot roast. It's equally good at room temperature and hot.

SERVES 6

2 cans (15 ounces each) sliced beets, with liquid

2 tablespoons peanut or safflower oil

1 cup coarsely chopped onion

2 tablespoons mild curry powder

1¼ cups coarse bulgur

1 tablespoon tomato paste

3 tablespoons pine nuts, toasted

Salt

2 tablespoons chopped fresh parsley, for serving

Drain the beets into a 4-cup liquid measuring cup. Add enough water to the beet liquid to equal 2½ cups. Set aside.

Heat the oil in a heavy 3-quart Dutch oven over medium-high heat.

Cook the onion, stirring occasionally, until lightly browned, about 3 minutes. Add the curry powder and bulgur and cook, stirring continuously, for 2 minutes. Stir in the tomato paste and cook for another 30 seconds.

Stir in the reserved beet liquid mixture and bring to a boil over high heat. Cover and cook over low heat until the liquid is absorbed, about 15 minutes. Turn off the heat. Let the bulgur sit undisturbed for 5 minutes.

Stir in the beets and pine nuts. Add salt to taste. Reheat over low heat, if necessary. Garnish with parsley just before serving.

OTHER IDEAS

• Use whole beets instead of sliced, or use 1 can of each to vary appearance.
• Use chopped, toasted pecans instead of pine nuts.
• Garnish with toasted unsweetened coconut or chopped fresh cilantro instead of parsley.

mashed millet with cauliflower and carrots

This recipe calls for millet grits, which are nothing more than the whole grain cracked into tiny bits. Grits take about 50 percent less time to cook and are ideal in this mashed dish. You can easily make the grits at home (see below) if you have difficulty buying them.

Since the millet and cauliflower are off-white, I've added some carrot for color—and also to sweeten the mix.

Serve this winning combo in place of mashed potatoes. No, it's nothing like them, except for the fact that you want to keep eating more.

SERVES 6 TO 8

1 cup millet grits or whole millet

1 large head of cauliflower (about 2½ pounds)

2 tablespoons (¼ stick) unsalted butter

2 teaspoons minced dried onion

1½ teaspoons dried tarragon

3 cups low-sodium chicken or vegetable broth

1 teaspoon salt, plus more to taste

1 cup grated carrot

½ to 1 cup milk

If using whole millet, grind it to grits in three or four batches in a spice grinder. It's fine if the grits are unevenly ground. Set aside.

Remove any outer leaves, and quarter the head of cauliflower. Slice off the central core, then chop finely by hand or by pulsing in a food processor. Set aside.

Melt 1 tablespoon of the butter in a 12-inch sauté pan or heavy skillet over medium heat. Stir in the onion and tarragon and cook for 20 seconds.

Add the broth, millet, and salt. Cover, and bring to a boil over high heat. Reduce the heat to medium and cook, covered, for 8 minutes.

Distribute the cauliflower and carrot on top. (Do not stir them in; the millet cooks best when surrounded by liquid.) Cover, lower the heat slightly, and continue cooking until the water is absorbed and the millet and vegetables are tender, 12 to 14 minutes. If the mixture becomes dry before the millet or vegetables are done, stir in ½ to 1 cup water, cover, and continue cooking another few minutes.

Turn the heat to medium. Stir in the remaining tablespoon butter and enough milk to make the mixture slightly soupy. Cook uncovered until the milk has been absorbed by the millet. Add more salt, if needed.

• Omit the tarragon and substitute 2 teaspoons mild curry powder.
• Use buttermilk instead of milk.
• Stir in 1 cup frozen peas along with the milk.

Millet-Cauliflower Pancakes: For each packed cup of the cooked mixture, blend in 1 large beaten egg, 1 tablespoon flour, and some chopped fresh herbs or chives, if you have them on hand. Season generously with salt and pepper. Heat a thin slick of hot oil on a griddle. Spoon heaping tablespoons onto the griddle and flatten into 3-inch pancakes. Brown well on both sides. Serve with a tiny dollop of sour cream or plain yogurt. One cup of "mash" yields 4 or 5 pancakes.

Millet Casserole with Cheese: Combine leftovers in a microwaveable casserole dish with halved cherry tomatoes and shredded Cheddar or Gruyère cheese. Set a paper towel on top. Microwave until the mixture is hot and the cheese is melted.

smoked paprika oats with peas

I hope that this quick and savory preparation of rolled oats will convince you that's it's a good idea to take oatmeal beyond the breakfast category. This recipe creates a soft and comforting side dish—a good choice to stand in for mashed potatoes. Or serve it with a savory omelet and salad for a light supper.

Smoked Spanish paprika, with its complex flavor and striking burnished color, is a great boon to busy cooks. Until recently it was not well known in America, but it's now widely available.

SERVES 4

2 cups oatmeal (old-fashioned rolled oats)

1½ tablespoons unsalted butter or olive oil

¾ to 1 teaspoon smoked Spanish paprika, to taste

Pinch of granulated garlic

Scant ½ teaspoon salt

½ cup frozen peas

1¾ cups low-sodium chicken broth

½ cup walnuts, toasted and coarsely chopped

Set a heavy 3-quart Dutch oven over medium-high heat. Add the oatmeal and toast it, stirring frequently, until it becomes aromatic, about 2 minutes.

Push the oats to one side of the pot and add the butter to the empty side. As the butter melts, stir in the paprika, garlic, and salt. Stir the seasoned butter into the oats.

Stir in the peas and broth. Bring to a boil. Cover, turn off the heat, and let sit until the liquid has been absorbed, about 5 minutes. Stir in the walnuts and serve.

OTHER IDEAS

- Use fresh or frozen corn kernels instead of the peas.
- Add freshly ground black pepper, to taste.

quinoa-creamed spinach

Quinoa flakes release a creamy starch as they cook, resulting in a dish that brings creamed spinach to mind. My devoted recipe-testing friend, Cathy Roberts, claims, "It's the best creamed spinach I've ever had! I could eat bowls of this."

The dish is amazingly fast, amazingly good, and elegant enough to serve company. Despite the elegance, it's also a very comforting side dish. Try it with the Oat-Crusted Turkey Cutlets with Gingered Cranberry Relish (page 74), as shown in the photo insert, or make a puddle of the spinach and top it with a few slices of grilled or baked chicken breast.

SERVES 4 TO 6

1 cup quinoa flakes

¾ teaspoon salt, plus more to taste

10 ounces fresh spinach, trimmed and coarsely chopped

1 tablespoon unsalted butter or olive oil

Freshly grated nutmeg

SPEED TIP: To reduce total prep time to under five minutes, use a bag of prewashed spinach.

Bring 3 cups of water to a rapid boil in a heavy 3-quart saucepan over medium-high heat. Stir in the quinoa flakes and salt.

Quickly set the spinach on top. Cover, reduce the heat slightly, and cook until the quinoa and spinach are tender, about 2 minutes. Turn off the heat. Stir in the butter, nutmeg to taste, and additional salt, if needed.

polenta-style quinoa

High-protein quinoa makes a fetching alternative to cornmeal in this porridgy side, good with grilled or broiled fish, steak, or chicken.

SERVES 3 TO 4

---

1 cup quinoa

¼ cup grated Parmesan cheese, plus more for serving

¼ cup grated Pecorino Romano

1 tablespoon unsalted butter

1 teaspoon chopped fresh rosemary

Salt and freshly ground black pepper

In a heavy 2-quart saucepan, bring 2 cups of water and the quinoa to a boil. Cover and cook over medium heat until the quinoa is tender (there should be no opaque white dot in the center) and most or all of the water has been absorbed, 12 to 15 minutes.

Stir in the Parmesan, Pecorino Romano, butter, rosemary, and salt and pepper to taste. Serve in small bowls dusted with extra Parmesan.

OTHER IDEAS
• Use low-sodium chicken or vegetable broth instead of water.
• Substitute 3 tablespoons chopped fresh parsley or basil for the rosemary.

parmesan
brown rice

Cooked in broth and seasoned with Italian herbs and Parmesan cheese, brown rice is transformed into a side dish with an Italian identity. Like risotto, it complements many types of entrées, including broiled chops, osso bucco, or even pot roast.

SERVES 4 TO 6

3 cups Minute brown rice

2¼ cups low-sodium chicken broth

1 teaspoon dried Italian herb blend

¼ cup finely chopped sun-dried tomatoes
   packed in oil

3 tablespoons grated Parmesan cheese, plus
   more for serving

2 tablespoons chopped fresh parsley, plus more
   for serving

¼ cup pine nuts, toasted

Salt and freshly ground black pepper

Set a heavy 3-quart Dutch oven over medium heat. Add the rice and toast, stirring occasionally, until it is aromatic, 3 to 5 minutes.

Slowly pour in the broth. Cover, reduce the heat, and simmer for 5 minutes. Stir in the Italian herbs and sun-dried tomatoes. Turn off the heat and let sit undisturbed for 5 minutes.

Stir in the Parmesan, parsley, pine nuts, and salt and pepper to taste.

OTHER IDEAS

• **Add ¼ to ½ teaspoon crushed red pepper flakes with the dried herbs.**

• **Use Romano cheese instead of Parmesan, or half of each.**

• **Add ½ cup toasted, chopped hazelnuts instead of pine nuts.**

• **To create a main dish, toss diced roast chicken, pork, or lamb into the cooked rice.**

rye flakes with buttermilk, caraway, and dill

Rye flakes are made by steaming and rolling whole-grain rye kernels. They are rye's version of oatmeal. Although they have none of the sourness we associate with rye bread, the flecks of caraway bring the bread to mind when you are eating this moist, stuffinglike side dish.

Serve it with goulash or a wintery beef borscht—or anything else you associate with the Eastern European kitchen.

SERVES 4

½ tablespoon unsalted butter

½ teaspoon caraway seeds, finely chopped

1 cup well-shaken buttermilk, plus more if needed

2 scallions, thinly sliced (keep white and green parts separate)

¼ teaspoon salt

1¾ cups rye flakes

3 tablespoons chopped fresh dill

Freshly ground black pepper

In a heavy 2-quart Dutch oven, melt the butter over medium heat. Stir in the caraway seeds and toast for 30 seconds.

Stir in the buttermilk, ¾ cup of water, the scallion whites, and salt. Bring to a boil over high heat. Use a whisk to reblend the liquid if the buttermilk floats to the top.

Stir in the rye flakes. Cover and reduce the heat. Simmer until the water is absorbed and the flakes are tender but still a little chewy, about 5 minutes.

Stir in the scallion greens, dill, plus salt and pepper to taste.

OTHER IDEAS

- Substitute barley, spelt, or Kamut flakes for the rye.
- Use snipped chives instead of scallions.
- Add ¼ cup dried currants and 2 tablespoons more water along with the rye flakes.

wild rice with mushrooms, potatoes, and squash

Quick-cooking wild rice, which is done in 10 minutes, has none of the unpredictability of standard wild rice, which can take anywhere from 40 to 90 minutes to cook. Here I combine the wild rice with the golds, reds, and oranges reminiscent of fall leaves in Vermont to create a celebratory dish, both hearty and beautiful. Try serving it with your next Thanksgiving turkey or with turkey burgers, for a casual supper.

SERVES 4 TO 6

2½ tablespoons olive oil

10 ounces cremini or button mushrooms, sliced

½ teaspoon salt, plus more to taste

1 small butternut squash (about 1 pound), peeled, seeded, and cut into ½-inch dice

1 large red-skinned potato (12 ounces), scrubbed and cut into ½-inch diced

1¼ cups instant wild rice

Heat 2 tablespoons of the oil in a heavy 4-quart Dutch oven over medium-high heat. Add the mushrooms and sprinkle with ½ teaspoon salt. Cook uncovered, stirring occasionally, until the mushrooms give up their liquid and are tender, 4 to 5 minutes. Transfer the mushrooms to a bowl.

Add the remaining ½ tablespoon oil to the pot and swirl it to coat the bottom. Add the squash, cover, and cook undisturbed for 2 minutes. Stir the squash and scrape up any browned bits sticking to the bottom of the pot. Stir in the potato, cover, and cook for 1 more minute. If the vegetables threaten to burn, proceed to the next step immediately.

Stir in 2 cups of water and bring to a boil over high heat. Stir in the rice. Cover and cook over medium heat until the rice, squash, and potatoes are tender, about 10 minutes. Stir in the mushrooms. Adjust the seasonings and serve.

OTHER IDEAS

• Instead of red-skinned potatoes, try peeled purple potatoes or scrubbed fingerlings.

• Substitute quick-cooking barley for the wild rice. Reduce the water to 1½ cups.

• Use half wild rice and half Minute brown rice.

breakfast
and quick
breads

four-grain porridge mix

It's fun (and economical) to make your own porridge mix. Here is one suggested formula, but consider porridge mix an opportunity to use up small amounts of leftover uncooked grains in whatever amounts you have. Just be sure that those you use cook in 20 minutes or less.

MAKES 2 CUPS

½ cup millet grits or whole millet

½ cup coarse bulgur

½ cup untoasted buckwheat (kasha)

½ cup barley flakes

1 cup raisins

1 teaspoon ground cinnamon

If you are using whole millet, grind it into coarse grits in two or three batches by pulsing in a spice grinder. It's fine if the grits are unevenly ground.

Combine the millet, bulgur, buckwheat, barley flakes, raisins, and cinnamon in a 1-quart zipper-top bag. Seal and toss gently to blend. Refrigerate in a tightly sealed container for up to 3 months.

OTHER IDEAS

• Use quick-cooking barley instead of barley flakes.

• Use any kind of rolled grain instead of the barley flakes.

• Substitute toasted buckwheat (kasha) for the untoasted buckwheat groats.

• Try dried cherries, chopped prunes, dates, or figs instead of the raisins.

• Add ⅓ cup ground flax seeds to the mix. They will produce a slightly gummy porridge.

good morning porridge

What ever happened to slow-cooked porridge? Once we got used to cold cereal and instant oatmeal, porridge went the way of unsliced bread.

Well, now that we can once again get a wholesome unsliced whole-wheat loaf, I'm hopeful that porridge will also make a comeback. There's nothing like it for giving yourself a soulful, loving start to the day.

SERVES 2

½ cup Four-Grain Porridge Mix (page 156)

Pinch of salt

⅓ cup milk

Brown sugar, maple syrup, or honey

⅓ cup plain or fruit yogurt

SPEED TIP: Since this porridge takes about 25 minutes to cook, make it for the first time on a leisurely weekend morning. Then, if you like it, double or triple the recipe the next time, refrigerate leftovers, and reheat portions before rushing out of the house on weekdays.

Combine the porridge mix and salt with 1¾ cups of water in a heavy 2-quart saucepan. Cover and bring to a boil over medium-high heat.

Reduce the heat, cover, and cook over medium heat until the liquid is absorbed, 13 to 15 minutes. Stir occasionally during this time to avoid lumps.

Add the milk and boil gently, uncovered, until the mixture thickens, the grains are tender, and most of the liquid has evaporated, 5 to 10 minutes longer.

Sweeten to taste with brown sugar. Garnish with a dollop of yogurt.

OTHER IDEAS

• For a richer porridge, use milk instead of all or part of the water. Take care to avoid boil-overs.

• Instead of dairy milk, use almond, rice, oat, or soy milk.

• Sweeten with strawberry or raspberry preserves instead of the suggested sweeteners.

• Instead of or in addition to yogurt, garnish with toasted, slivered almonds.

millet grits with prunes, ginger, and sunflower seeds

Millet makes an appealing, hearty breakfast cereal when toasted and then dressed up with honey and spice and everything nice. Consider preparing it when you have a visitor who is on a gluten-free diet.

SERVES 4 TO 6

1 cup millet grits or whole millet

¼ teaspoon ground cinnamon

Pinch of ground allspice

½ teaspoon salt

⅓ cup tightly packed chopped or snipped pitted prunes

2 tablespoons chopped, crystallized ginger

½ cup half-and-half or whole or 2% milk

1 to 2 tablespoons unsalted butter, to taste

Honey or brown sugar

¼ cup shelled, unsalted sunflower seeds, toasted

> **SPEED TIP:** By using grits rather than the whole grain, you cut the cooking time almost in half.

If you are using whole millet, grind it into coarse grits in two or three batches by pulsing in a spice grinder. It's fine if the grits are unevenly ground.

In a heavy 3-quart saucepan, toast the millet over medium heat, stirring frequently, until aromatic, about 3 minutes. Stir in the cinnamon and allspice.

Gradually stir in 5 cups of water and the salt. Bring to a boil over high heat.

Cover and simmer for 15 minutes, stirring occasionally to prevent the grits from settling to the bottom.

Stir in the prunes and crystallized ginger. Cook uncovered at a gentle boil, stirring occasionally, until the porridge is thick and the millet is tender—it will remain slightly grainy, even when thoroughly cooked—3 to 10 minutes more, depending upon the size of the grits.

Stir in the half-and-half, butter, and honey to taste. Stir uncovered over medium heat until the mixture develops a porridgelike consistency, 3 to 5 minutes. Stir in the sunflower seeds, reserving a few for garnish.

Spoon into bowls, sprinkle with the remaining sunflower seeds, and drizzle with honey, if you wish.

OTHER IDEAS

- **Cook in half milk and half water. Omit the half-and-half.**
- **Substitute raisins or dried cranberries for the prunes.**

Millet Pancakes: Blend a lightly beaten egg into 1 cup of leftover porridge. If needed, stir in enough milk to create the consistency of pancake batter. Cook on a hot skillet as for pancakes.

Wheatena Revisited

Remember Wheatena? For some of us, its deep toasty aroma brings back fond memories of family breakfasts in the fifties.

Wheatena is made from toasted crushed whole wheat, and the porridge cooks in under 5 minutes—an early version of an instant breakfast.

No one talked about the health-promoting benefits of eating whole grains in those days. We were too busy eating our Wheatena.

Serves 2

⅔ cup Wheatena

⅛ teaspoon salt (optional)

Over high heat, bring 1¾ cups of water, the Wheatena, and salt (if using) to a rapid boil in a heavy 1- or 2-quart pot.

Reduce the heat and cook at a gentle boil, stirring occasionally, until the porridge reaches the desired consistency, 4 to 5 minutes.

Serve immediately or cover until needed. Stir before serving.

OTHER IDEAS

Make it with half milk and half water.

Sweeten with honey, maple syrup, or brown sugar.

Cook the cereal with raisins or chopped, dried fruit.

Serve with a dollop of yogurt on top.

my favorite oatmeal

I've been having a morning love affair with "my oatmeal" for quite a while. My version steeps in a ratio of only 1 part water to 1 part old-fashioned oats. This frugal amount of liquid results in rolled oats that keep their shape and have a pleasantly chewy texture.

Even though it takes only 5 minutes to prepare, I usually make enough to last for the week. Each morning I plop my daily portion of the cooked cereal into a bowl, cover it with milk or vanilla soy milk, and get it piping hot in the microwave.

I stir in a few tablespoons of heart-healthy ground flax seeds and chopped walnuts, and then stir in a little maple syrup. Often I add chopped apples in winter and peaches or nectarines in summer.

This, for me, is a very comforting and delicious way to start the day.

MAKES 5 TO 6 PORTIONS

---

2 cups oatmeal (old-fashioned rolled oats)

Bring 2 cups of water to a boil in a heavy 2-quart pot. Stir in the oats. Cover and turn off the heat. Let steep for 5 minutes. Uncover and let cool in the pot. Transfer to an airtight container and refrigerate for up to 1 week.

OTHER IDEAS
- **Try a mixture of barley flakes, wheat flakes, and rolled oats.**
- **Steep the oats in milk rather than water.**

oatmeal-on-the-go

It's easy to make your own oatmeal-to-go if you have a small widemouthed thermos. Spoon the mix listed below into the thermos and pour boiling water over it. Screw the cover on, and by the time you get to work your oatmeal will be ready to eat.

To make a batch of mix in advance, just triple or quadruple the recipe and scoop out ¾ cup of dry mix for your daily portion.

SERVES 1

½ cup oatmeal (old-fashioned rolled oats)

2 tablespoons slivered almonds, toasted

1 heaping tablespoon raisins

1 to 2 teaspoons sugar, to taste

⅛ teaspoon ground cinnamon

Pinch of salt

Combine the oats, almonds, raisins, sugar, cinnamon, and salt in a small, widemouthed thermos. Pour in ½ cup boiling water for firm oatmeal or ⅔ cup for soft, loose oatmeal. Immediately screw on the top and shake gently. Wait at least 5 minutes before eating.

OTHER IDEAS
- **Add boiling milk instead of water.**

chai-spiced oatmeal

It's tasty and fun to gussy up oatmeal with the spices we associate with chai tea. Both oatmeal and tea bring to mind comfort and relaxation, welcome benefits in our busy lives.

Cooking the oatmeal in only 1¼ cups of milk results in chewy oat flakes enveloped in a sweet, gently spiced coating.

SERVES 2

1¼ cups milk, plus more for serving

1 to 2 tablespoons honey, to taste

½ tablespoon unsalted butter

½ teaspoon pumpkin pie spice, or ⅛ teaspoon each ground ginger, cardamom, cinnamon, and nutmeg

⅛ teaspoon ground cardamom

⅛ teaspoon salt, plus more to taste

1 cup oatmeal (old-fashioned rolled oats)

½ teaspoon vanilla extract

Pour the milk into a heavy 2-quart saucepan and set over medium-high heat. Stir in 1 tablespoon of the honey, the butter, pumpkin pie spice, cardamom, and salt.

Once the milk is boiling, turn off the heat to avoid boil-overs. Quickly stir in the oatmeal. Cover and simmer over low heat until most of the milk has been absorbed, 8 to 9 minutes. Stir in the vanilla.

Stir in additional honey, if needed. Serve hot in bowls. Pour extra milk on top, if you wish.

OTHER IDEAS

• For a creamier version, increase the milk to 2 cups and cook for 11 to 14 minutes. For the last few minutes, cook uncovered while stirring.

• Add ¼ cup raisins, dried cranberries, or chopped dried apricot along with the spices.

• Add 1 teaspoon finely chopped fresh ginger with the oatmeal.

• Garnish each portion with a light sprinkling of brown sugar and toasted walnuts.

whole-grain pancake mix

It's so easy and economical to toss together a pancake mix that I find myself wondering why we ever got into the habit of buying prepared mixes.

Feel free to double the mix if you are cooking for a family of pancake lovers.

MAKES 3¾ CUPS, ENOUGH FOR 3 BATCHES OF WHEAT AND OAT PANCAKES (SEE PAGE 164)

2½ cups whole-wheat pastry flour

1 cup oatmeal (old-fashioned rolled oats)

¼ cup sugar

1 tablespoon baking powder

1½ teaspoons baking soda

¾ teaspoon salt

In a large zipper-top bag, combine the flour, oats, sugar, baking powder, baking soda, and salt. Seal and shake gently until thoroughly mixed. Label and date the bag.

Refrigerate for up to 3 months. Shake gently to aerate the mix before each use.

OTHER IDEAS

- **Use spelt flour instead of whole-wheat pastry flour.**

wheat and oat pancakes

I love the gentle sweetness and faint nuttiness of whole-grain pancakes. With the judicious use of leaveners like baking powder and soda, they are as light and fluffy as those made of refined flour.

This recipe makes about sixteen 2½-inch pancakes. If you don't need that many, refrigerate the unused batter for up to 3 days, then thin it with extra buttermilk and stir in a pinch of baking soda before making a second batch.

Alternatively, use up all of the batter and refrigerate extra pancakes. Rewarm them in the oven. It's fun to serve these pancakes for a casual supper along with some grilled sausages.

SERVES 4

1 large egg

1 cup well-shaken buttermilk, plus more if needed

2 tablespoons (¼ stick) unsalted butter, melted

1 teaspoon vanilla extract

1¼ cups Whole-Grain Pancake Mix (page 163; stir before measuring)

Optional Additions

½ cup dried currants or blueberries

⅓ cup shelled, unsalted sunflower or pumpkin seeds

Grated zest of 1 lemon or orange

¼ teaspoon ground cinnamon

Safflower or canola oil, for greasing the griddle

Maple syrup or honey, for serving

OTHER IDEAS

Apple-Spice Pancakes: Omit the cinnamon, and add ½ teaspoon pumpkin pie spice to the dry ingredients for 1 batch. Add 1 cup finely chopped, unpeeled tart apple when you stir the wet and dry ingredients together.

Berry-Orange Pancakes: Omit the cinnamon and stir ½ teaspoon ground cardamom into the dry ingredients for 1 batch. Add 1 cup fresh or frozen blueberries or raspberries, and the grated zest of 1 orange when you stir the wet and dry ingredients together.

Pear-Ginger Pancakes: Add 3 tablespoons finely chopped crystallized ginger and 1 cup finely chopped, unpeeled ripe pear when you stir the wet and dry ingredients together.

If you plan to keep the pancakes warm so that you can serve them all at once, preheat the oven to 200°F.

In a large bowl, lightly beat the egg. Blend in the buttermilk, butter, and vanilla.

Fold in the pancake mix and any optional additions just until the flour is absorbed. Avoid overmixing.

Heat a large griddle or skillet over medium heat. Lightly coat the surface with oil. When a drop of water thrown on the griddle immediately sizzles, pour on ⅛ cup (2 tablespoons) batter per pancake, allowing space for the batter to spread.

When the pancakes are dry around the edges and the bottoms are nicely browned, 2 to 3 minutes, flip them. Cook until browned on the second side, 1 to 2 minutes longer. Lower the heat if the pancakes are browning too quickly, leaving the center undercooked.

Serve each batch as soon as it's done, arranging the pancakes slightly overlapped. Do not stack the pancakes—this causes them to steam and become soggy.

If you prefer to bake and serve all of the pancakes at once, set them in a single layer on a baking pan and place in the warm oven.

Accompany the pancakes with maple syrup or honey.

whole-grain
waffle mix

When I was a kid, we ate waffles every Sunday morning. It's a worthy tradition that is easy to make happen with this mix on hand.

MAKES 4 CUPS, ENOUGH FOR 4 BATCHES OF SPELT BUTTERMILK WAFFLES (SEE PAGE 167)

3 cups spelt flour

1 cup cornmeal

2 teaspoons salt

1 tablespoon baking powder

1 teaspoon baking soda

1 teaspoon ground cinnamon (optional)

In a large zipper-top bag, combine the flour, cornmeal, salt, baking powder, baking soda, and cinnamon (if using). Shake gently or stir to blend the ingredients thoroughly. Label and date the bag.

Refrigerate for up to 3 months. Shake gently to aerate the mix before each use.

OTHER IDEAS

• **Instead of spelt flour, use white whole-wheat flour or whole-wheat pastry flour.**

• **Replace the cinnamon with ½ teaspoon ground cardamom.**

spelt buttermilk waffles

I have a small electric waffle iron and often make waffles when I have friends over for a weekend brunch. I usually just serve them one by one, fresh out of the waffler. The alternative is to keep the waffles warm in a 200°F oven and serve them all at once.

I often make a double batch, bake all of the batter, and freeze extra. I pop a frozen waffle in my toaster oven for a weekday breakfast treat.

MAKES THREE 6-INCH ROUND WAFFLES

1 large egg

1 cup well-shaken buttermilk

3 tablespoons safflower or canola oil

2 tablespoons honey

1 cup Whole-Grain Waffle Mix (page 166; stir before measuring)

¼ cup sunflower seeds, 2 tablespoons minced crystallized ginger, or 3 tablespoons dried currants (optional)

Butter or oil, for greasing the waffle iron

Maple syrup, fruit preserves, or honey, for serving

In a large bowl, lightly beat the egg. Blend in the buttermilk, oil, and honey.

Stir in the waffle mix and any optional additions just until the flour is absorbed. Avoid overmixing.

Heat a waffle iron according to the manufacturer's instructions. Add enough butter to cover the lower grid by half to two-thirds. Bake until crisp, usually 4 to 5 minutes.

Accompany the hot waffles with maple syrup, fruit preserves, or honey.

OTHER IDEAS

• Use melted butter instead of oil.

• Replace honey with agave syrup.

• Add to the batter 1½ teaspoons chopped, fresh rosemary and the grated zest of 1 lemon.

• Serve the waffles topped with blueberries or diced strawberries.

savory mini-loaf mix

Having this mix on hand allows you to make savory quick breads in about a half hour, since they require no rising time and are baked in small pans.

The mix is based on white whole-wheat flour, which produces lightly colored and pleasantly textured baked goods.

MAKES ABOUT 9¼ CUPS, ENOUGH FOR
3 BATCHES OF MINI-LOAVES

9 cups white whole-wheat flour, such as King
    Arthur's
3 tablespoons baking powder
1½ teaspoons baking soda
1 tablespoon plus ¾ teaspoon salt

In a 1-gallon zipper-top bag, combine the flour, baking powder, baking soda, and salt. Seal. Shake gently or stir to blend ingredients thoroughly. Label and date the bag.

Refrigerate or freeze for up to 4 months. Stir well to aerate the mix before measuring for each use.

OTHER IDEAS
• **Use spelt flour instead of white whole wheat.**

savory mini-loaves

Baking whole-grain batters in small loaf pans—about 5 x 3 x 2 inches—has two advantages: it reduces baking time substantially and ensures even cooking.

If you don't own mini-loaf pans, or want to give the loaves as gifts, purchase the heavy foil ones available in most supermarkets.

These loaves look quite charming and are a fetching last-minute alternative to yeasted bread.

MAKES 4 MINI-LOAVES

Olive oil, for coating the pans (optional)

2 tablespoons flour, for coating the pans (optional)

1 large egg

1¾ cups well-shaken buttermilk, plus more if needed

¼ cup olive oil

2 tablespoons honey

3 cups Savory Mini-Loaf Mix (page 168; stir before measuring)

Place a rack in the middle of the oven and preheat the oven to 375°F. If your four mini-loaf pans aren't nonstick, brush the bottoms and sides lightly with oil, and coat lightly with the flour. Tip out any excess flour.

Beat the egg in a large bowl. Blend in the buttermilk, oil, and honey.

Fold the Mini-Loaf Mix into the liquid. Add a few tablespoons more buttermilk if the mixture appears dry and there is some unabsorbed flour. Do not overmix.

Divide the dough among the four prepared loaf pans. Use a knife or spatula to smooth out the tops. Set the pans on a cookie sheet. Bake for 12 minutes. Rotate the cookie sheet. Continue baking until the tops are brown and a cake tester inserted in the center comes out dry, 8 to 10 minutes longer.

Transfer the mini-loaves to a cooling rack. Let cool for 10 minutes. Unmold. Serve warm or at room temperature. Slice with a serrated-edged bread knife.

OTHER IDEAS

Italian Mini-Loaves: Stir 2 teaspoons dried Italian herb blend, 1 teaspoon granulated garlic, and ½ teaspoon crushed red pepper flakes into the mini-loaf mix for one batch. Before baking, sprinkle Parmesan or Romano cheese on top of each loaf.

Southwestern Mini-Loaves: Stir 2 teaspoons chili powder, 1 teaspoon each onion powder, dried oregano leaves, and chopped cumin seeds, and ½ teaspoon ground chipotle (optional) into the mini-loaf mix for one batch. Before baking, gently press untoasted pumpkin seeds into the top of each loaf.

buttermilk biscuit mix

Something about being served a basket of homemade, freshly baked biscuits delights people and makes them feel especially cared for. And it's so easy to do, once you have a mix on hand and a recipe that requires no special equipment.

MAKES ABOUT 6¾ CUPS, ENOUGH FOR 3 BATCHES OF BISCUITS

4½ cups whole-wheat pastry flour

2 cups oatmeal (old-fashioned rolled oats)

2 tablespoons baking powder

2 tablespoons sugar

1½ teaspoons baking soda

1½ teaspoons salt

In a 1-gallon zipper-top bag, combine the flour, oatmeal, baking powder, sugar, baking soda, and salt. Shake gently or stir to blend ingredients thoroughly. Label and date the bag.

Refrigerate or freeze for up to 4 months. Stir well to aerate the mix before measuring for each use.

buttermilk biscuits

This biscuit recipe is quite versatile. You can freeze the shaped dough and bake the biscuits as needed, adding a few minutes to the cooking time. Or you can even freeze the biscuits after they are baked and have cooled to room temperature.

Serve the biscuits with a soup or stew, or stuff them with thinly sliced ham or cheese and offer them when you're serving cocktails. Alternatively, serve them with butter and jam for brunch.

MAKES 9 BISCUITS

2¼ cups Buttermilk Biscuit Mix (page 170; stir before measuring)

6 tablespoons (¾ stick) cold unsalted butter, cut into bits

2 to 3 tablespoons whole-wheat pastry flour, for kneading the dough

¾ cup well-shaken buttermilk

Set a rack in the bottom third of the oven and preheat the oven to 450°F. Use a large nonstick baking sheet or line a baking sheet with parchment.

Place the biscuit mix in a bowl. Add the butter and work it into the flour with a pastry blender, two knives, or your fingers until the mixture resembles coarse meal.

Stir in the buttermilk. Lightly dust a clean, flat surface with the flour. Turn the dough (it will be loose and moist) onto the surface and knead about ten times to form a cohesive mass. Knead in another 1 tablespoon of flour if the dough is too sticky to work with or sticks to the surface.

Pat the dough into a square about 1 inch thick. Cut into 9 squares. Using a spatula, arrange the squares on a baking sheet, leaving a little space between them.

Bake for 8 minutes. Rotate the pan and bake until a cake tester inserted into the center comes out dry and the biscuits feel firm to the touch, about 6 minutes.

Serve immediately. Alternatively, cool on a rack and freeze in an airtight container for up to 2 months.

OTHER IDEAS

Sage-Cheddar Biscuits: Add 2 teaspoons dried, crumbled sage to the dry biscuit mix for one batch. Stir in ¼ cup shredded sharp Cheddar cheese when you add the buttermilk.

Cranberry-Pecan Biscuits: Stir in ⅓ cup each chopped dried cranberries and chopped pecans when you add the buttermilk. Dust the tops lightly with sugar before baking.

basic scone mix

*Ah scones . . . They seem so special and yet
they are so easy to make. Having a mix at the
ready makes it easy to enjoy freshly baked scones
on a whim.*

MAKES 6 CUPS, ENOUGH FOR 3 BATCHES

5 cups whole-wheat pastry or white whole-
   wheat flour
1 cup sugar
1½ tablespoons baking powder
1¼ teaspoons salt

SPEED TIP: The mix, the dough, and the baked
scones all freeze beautifully, so you can be all set
at every step.

Combine the flour, sugar, baking powder, and salt in
a 1-gallon zipper-top bag. Stir well or shake gently to
evenly distribute the ingredients. Label and date
the bag.

Refrigerate or freeze for up to 4 months. Stir well
before measuring for each batch.

cran-apple scones

This scone looks fairly traditional but surprises with its sweet hint of licorice fennel seeds. It's a treat to have for breakfast or an afternoon snack.

Please resist any temptation to substitute low-fat milk for the heavy cream; the texture won't be nearly as good.

MAKES 8 SCONES

2 cups Basic Scone Mix (page 172; stir before measuring)

1 teaspoon grated orange zest

½ teaspoon fennel seeds, chopped (optional)

5 tablespoons cold unsalted butter, cut into bits

1 large egg

3 tablespoons heavy cream or half-and-half

1 cup finely diced unpeeled apple

⅓ cup dried cranberries, coarsely chopped

2 to 3 tablespoons shelled, unsalted sunflower seeds

Place a rack in the upper third of the oven, and preheat the oven to 375°F.

Place the scone mix in a large bowl. Stir in the orange zest and fennel seeds. Add the butter and work it into the flour with a pastry blender, two knives, or your fingers until the mixture resembles coarse meal.

In a small bowl, beat the egg with a fork, and blend in the cream. Add the liquid ingredients, apple, and cranberries to the dry ingredients and stir just until the dry ingredients are moistened. At this point, the dough should be crumbly; do not overmix.

Turn the dough out onto a flat, dry surface. Gently knead the dough into a mass, incorporating any loose bits as you go. Shape the dough into a disc about 6 inches in diameter and ¾ inch thick. Cut into 8 wedges. Scatter and then gently press the sunflower seeds into the tops. With a spatula, transfer the scones to an ungreased baking sheet, leaving a little space between them.

Bake for 6 minutes. Rotate the pan. Continue baking until a toothpick inserted in the center comes out clean, 6 to 8 minutes longer. (The scones are likely to be pale.)

Serve warm, or let cool on a rack. Store in a well-sealed container at room temperature for 1 day or cool to room termpature and freeze for up to 4 months. For best taste and texture, serve warm.

lemon poppy
seed scones

These scones are especially delicious when split and slathered with raspberry jam.

MAKES 8 SCONES

2 cups Basic Scone Mix (page 172; stir before
    measuring)

2 tablespoons poppy seeds

5 tablespoons cold unsalted butter, cut into bits

1 large egg

2 teaspoons grated lemon zest

1½ tablespoons freshly squeezed lemon juice

2 tablespoons heavy cream or half-and-half

Place the oven rack in the upper third of the oven, and preheat the oven to 375°F.

Place the scone mix in a large bowl. Stir in the poppy seeds. With a pastry blender, two knives, or your fingers, cut the butter into the flour until the mixture resembles coarse meal.

In a small bowl, beat the egg with a fork, and blend in the lemon zest, juice, and cream. Add the liquid ingredients to the dry ingredients and stir just until the dry ingredients are moistened. The dough will be crumbly; do not overmix.

Turn the dough out onto a flat, dry surface. Gently knead the dough into a mass, incorporating any loose bits as you go. Shape the dough into a disc about 6 inches in diameter and ¾ inch thick. Cut the round into 8 wedges. Transfer the scones to an ungreased baking sheet, leaving a little space between them.

Bake for 6 minutes. Rotate the pan. Continue baking until a toothpick inserted in the center comes out clean, 6 to 8 minutes longer. (The scones are likely to be pale.)

Serve warm, or let the scones cool on a rack. Store in a well-sealed container at room temperature for 1 day or cool to room temperature and freeze for up to 4 months. For best taste and texture, serve warm.

chocolate chip–espresso scones

Lovers of chocolate and coffee are delighted by these elegant, dark scones—a special treat for brunch or an afternoon snack. Please resist any temptation to use any milk product that contains less fat than the half-and-half—that is, unless you won't object to a very coarsely textured and strongly wheaty-tasting scone.

MAKES 8 SCONES

2 cups Basic Scone Mix (page 172; stir before measuring)

2 tablespoons instant espresso powder or 2½ tablespoons espresso granules

5 tablespoons cold butter, cut into bits

1 large egg

¼ cup heavy cream or half-and-half

½ cup semisweet chocolate chips

3 tablespoons pine nuts

Place a rack in the upper third of the oven, and preheat the oven to 375°F.

Place the scone mix in a large bowl. Blend in the espresso powder. With a pastry blender, two knives, or your fingers, cut the butter into the flour until the mixture looks like coarse meal.

In a small bowl, beat the egg with a fork, and blend in the cream. Add the egg-cream mixture and the chocolate chips to the dry ingredients and mix just until the dry ingredients are moistened. The mixture will be crumbly; do not overmix.

Turn the dough out onto a flat, dry surface. Gently knead the dough into a mass, incorporating any loose bits as you go. Shape the dough into a disc about 6 inches in diameter and ¾ inch thick. Cut the round into 8 wedges. Gently press pine nuts into the tops. With a spatula, transfer the scones to an ungreased baking sheet, leaving a little space between them.

Bake for 6 minutes. Rotate the pan. Continue baking until a toothpick inserted in the center comes out clean, 6 to 8 minutes longer.

Transfer the scones from the pan to a rack. Store in a well-sealed container at room temperature for 1 day or cool to room temperature and freeze for up to 4 months. For best taste and texture, serve warm.

OTHER IDEAS
• **Instead of pine nuts, gently press ⅓ cup chocolate chips into the top. As soon as the scones come out of the oven, use a spatula to spread the chips out and create a frosting.**

wheat and oat muffin mix

The combination of wheat flour and oatmeal creates a light, moist muffin, the ideal base for a variety of flavorings.

MAKES 9¼ CUPS; ENOUGH FOR 3 BATCHES

---

5 cups whole-wheat pastry flour

2 cups oatmeal (old-fashioned rolled oats)

2¼ cups sugar

2 tablespoons baking powder

1 teaspoon baking soda

1½ teaspoons salt

Combine the flour, oatmeal, sugar, baking powder, baking soda, and salt in a 1-gallon zipper-top bag. Shake to distribute the ingredients. Seal and label the bag. Refrigerate or freeze until needed, up to 4 months.

fig-anise muffins with hazelnuts

Thanks to the generous addition of chopped figs, the batter for these muffins puffs out over the top to create charming "hats." For best results, use moist figs, not the leathery type strung on rope.

MAKES 12 MUFFINS

2 large eggs

¾ cups well-shaken buttermilk

½ cup safflower or canola oil plus 1 teaspoon
    for oiling muffin tins

1 teaspoon vanilla extract

½ teaspoon anise seeds, coarsely chopped

3 cups Wheat and Oat Muffin Mix (page 176;
    stir before measuring)

1 cup dried California mission figs, trimmed and
    chopped

⅔ cups coarsely chopped hazelnuts, toasted

2 tablespoons oatmeal (old-fashioned rolled
    oats), for garnish

Set a rack in the top third of the oven, and preheat the oven to 400°F. Brush 12 standard muffin cups—and around the top edges between the cups—lightly with oil. Set aside.

In a large bowl, lightly beat the eggs with a fork. Stir in the buttermilk, oil, vanilla, and anise seeds.

Add the muffin mix, figs, and nuts. Stir just until most of the flour is incorporated. Do not overmix.

Divide the batter among the prepared muffin cups. (They will be quite full.) Sprinkle the tops with oatmeal, and gently press it into the batter.

Bake for 7 minutes. Rotate the tin(s). Continue baking until the muffins spring back to a gentle touch and a cake tester inserted in the center comes out clean, 5 to 7 more minutes.

Set the tin(s) on a rack to cool for 10 minutes. Twist gently or run a knife around the edges to release the muffins. Eat warm, or cool to room temperature. If not eating the same day, freeze in a zipper-top freezer bag for up to 3 months. Thaw at room temperature or in the oven.

prune-cranberry muffins with crystallized ginger

Using ginger in both the powdered and crystallized form gives these muffins double the zing.

MAKES 12 MUFFINS

2 large eggs

¾ cups well-shaken buttermilk

½ cup safflower or canola oil plus 1 teaspoon for oiling muffin tins

1 teaspoon vanilla extract

3 cups Wheat and Oat Muffin Mix (page 176; stir before measuring)

1 teaspoon ground ginger

Grated zest of 1 lemon

¾ cup chopped, moist, pitted prunes

¼ cup plus 2 tablespoons sunflower seeds

¼ cup chopped dried cranberries

¼ cup chopped crystallized ginger

Set a rack in the top third of the oven and preheat the oven to 400°F. Brush 12 standard muffin cups and around the top edges between the cups lightly with oil. Set aside.

In a large bowl, lightly beat the eggs with a fork. Stir in the buttermilk, oil, and vanilla.

Add the muffin mix, ginger, lemon zest, prunes, ¼ cup sunflower seeds, cranberries, and crystallized ginger. Stir just until most of the flour is incorporated. Do not overmix.

Divide the batter among the prepared muffin cups. (They will be quite full.) Sprinkle some sunflower seeds onto the top of each muffin and very gently press them into the batter.

Bake for 7 minutes. Rotate the tin(s). Continue baking until the muffins spring back to a gentle touch and a cake tester inserted in the center comes out clean, 5 to 7 more minutes.

Set the tin(s) on a rack to cool for 10 minutes. Twist gently or run a knife around the edges to release the muffins. Eat warm, or cool to room temperature. If not eating the same day, freeze in a zipper-top freezer bag for up to 3 months. Thaw at room temperature or in the oven.

apricot-orange muffins

I don't often remember to combine apricots with the bright flavors of orange zest and cardamom, but when I do, I'm reminded that it's a very good idea.

MAKES 12 MUFFINS

2 large eggs

¾ cups well-shaken buttermilk

½ cup safflower or canola oil plus 1 teaspoon for oiling muffin tins

1 teaspoon vanilla extract

½ teaspoon ground cardamom

Grated zest of 1 orange

3 cups Wheat and Oat Muffin Mix (page 176; stir to aerate before measuring)

1 cup dried (moist) apricots, coarsely chopped or snipped

¼ cup unsalted, shelled pumpkin seeds

Set a rack in the top third of the oven and preheat the oven to 400°F. Brush 12 standard muffin cups and around the top edges between the cups lightly with oil. Set aside.

In a large bowl, lightly beat the eggs with a fork. Stir in the buttermilk, oil, and vanilla.

Add the cardamom, orange zest, muffin mix, and apricots. Stir just until the flour is incorporated. Do not overmix.

Divide the batter among the prepared muffin cups. (They will be quite full.) Sprinkle ½ teaspoon pumpkin seeds onto the top of each muffin, and gently press them into the batter.

Bake for 7 minutes. Rotate the tin(s). Continue baking until the muffins spring back to a gentle touch and a cake tester inserted in the center comes out clean, 5 to 7 more minutes.

Set the tin(s) on a rack to cool for 10 minutes. Twist gently or run a knife around the edges to release the muffins. Eat warm, or cool to room temperature. If not eating the same day, freeze in a zipper-topped freezer bag for up to 3 months. Thaw at room temperature or in the oven.

puddings, pies, cookies, and cakes

Buckwheat Indian Pudding

Bulgur Pudding with Figs and Crystallized Ginger

Granola Raspberry Parfait

Quinoa Banana Pudding with Dried Mango

Baked Oatmeal Pudding

Versatile Mix for Cookies, Crumbles, and Pie Crust

Peach Blueberry Crumble

> *Fresh Fruit Crumble*

> *Individual Fruit Crumbles*

Orange-Scented Chocolate Chip Cookies

> *Pecan Sandies*

> *Almond Cookies*

> *Lemon Pignoli Cookies with Rosemary*

Versatile Pie Crust

Chocolate Pudding Pie

Butterscotch Tapioca Pecan Pie

Banana Coconut Cream Pie

Fresh Fruit–Topped Cake Mix

Fresh Fruit–Topped Cake

buckwheat indian pudding

Nourishing buckwheat brings the nubbly texture of large pearl tapioca to mind in this sweet pudding—a warming cold-weather dessert flavored with molasses, ginger, and cinnamon and studded with raisins and walnuts. Serve it with a dollop of vanilla ice cream, sweetened whipped cream, or vanilla yogurt.

Leftovers are nice for breakfast or brunch.

SERVES 4

1 cup untoasted buckwheat

⅛ teaspoon salt

1 cup 2% milk

⅓ to ½ cup raisins

1 tablespoon unsalted butter

2 tablespoons molasses

1 to 3 tablespoons brown sugar to taste, plus
    more for serving

¾ teaspoon ground ginger

¾ teaspoon ground cinnamon

½ cup chopped walnuts, toasted

In a heavy 2-quart saucepan, bring 1½ cups water to a boil over high heat. Add the buckwheat and salt. Cover and reduce the heat to medium. Cook until most or all of the water has been absorbed, about 8 minutes.

Stir in the milk, raisins, butter, and molasses. Add the brown sugar, ginger, and cinnamon. Bring to a boil. Cook uncovered at a gentle boil, stirring occasionally, until the buckwheat is tender, the mixture thickens, and most of the milk has been absorbed, about 10 minutes.

Stir in the walnuts. Serve warm in small bowls.

OTHER IDEAS
• **For a richer dessert, cook the buckwheat in milk instead of water.**
• **Use dried cranberries instead of raisins, or half of each.**
• **Sweeten with maple syrup instead of brown sugar.**
• **Substitute 2 teaspoons minced fresh ginger for the dried.**

bulgur pudding with figs and crystallized ginger

Fine bulgur—commonly used in savory tabbouleh salads—makes an appealing base for a quick, sweet dessert pudding. For best results, choose soft, plump dried California figs, not the leathery Turkish figs strung on rope.

Serve this dessert hot or at room temperature, topped with ice cream or sweetened whipped cream. It's also great for breakfast.

SERVES 4 TO 6

2 to 3 tablespoons honey

⅛ teaspoon salt

¾ cup fine bulgur

1 cup (packed) dried figs (about 6 ounces), trimmed and chopped

¼ cup coarsely chopped crystallized ginger

1 cup 2% milk

½ cup dried cranberries

¼ teaspoon ground allspice

¼ cup pine nuts, toasted

In a heavy 3-quart saucepan, bring 1½ cups of water to a boil. Blend in 2 tablespoons of the honey and the salt. Stir in the bulgur, figs, and crystallized ginger. Cover and let stand off heat until most of the water is absorbed, about 5 minutes.

Stir in the milk, cranberries, allspice, and additional honey, if desired. Bring to a boil. Reduce the heat and simmer uncovered, stirring occasionally, until the mixture thickens to the consistency of oatmeal, 2 to 3 minutes. Cover and let sit until ready to serve.

Stir in the pine nuts, reserving a few to garnish each portion. Serve warm or at room temperature.

OTHER IDEAS

• **Use vanilla soy milk instead of cow milk. Since soy milk is already sweetened, add honey to taste toward the end of cooking instead of at the beginning.**

• **Substitute pitted prunes for the figs and dried cherries for the cranberries.**

granola
raspberry parfait

Here is a pretty, no-cook dessert to make when raspberries are in season. Simply layer your favorite granola with raspberries and jam-sweetened ricotta. Any granola made from rolled oats is automatically whole grain. Opt for an organic brand; Nature's Path is a personal favorite.

The resulting "parfait" is edible proof that granola needn't be restricted to the breakfast table. If you don't have parfait glasses for serving, use wine goblets or even clear tumblers.

SERVES 6

1½ cups low-fat ricotta

¼ cup low-fat, plain yogurt

4 tablespoons raspberry jam, or more to taste

1 teaspoon grated lemon zest

1½ cups whole-grain granola

1½ to 2 cups fresh or frozen (defrosted) raspberries

Fresh mint leaves, for serving (optional)

In a food processor, puree the ricotta, yogurt, jam, and lemon zest. Taste, and blend in more jam if you'd like the mixture to be sweeter.

Spoon 2 tablespoons of the granola into each glass. Top with 2 tablespoons of the ricotta mixture and a layer of raspberries. Repeat with a second layer of granola, ricotta, and raspberries. Garnish with a few mint leaves.

Serve immediately or refrigerate until needed, up to 6 hours.

OTHER IDEAS
• **Use half blueberries and half raspberries.**
• **Substitute 1 pound sliced strawberries for the raspberries. Use strawberry instead of raspberry jam.**

quinoa banana pudding with dried mango

Since quinoa is one of the most versatile, quick-cooking grains I know, I wasn't very surprised to discover that it makes a terrific base for a dessert pudding. Stirring mashed banana in at the end gives this luscious pudding creaminess without the cream.

Serve warm or chilled.

SERVES 6 TO 8

1½ cups quinoa

1 can (13.5 ounces) unsweetened coconut milk

¼ cup sugar, plus more to taste

Pinch of salt

½ cup dried mango slices, snipped into ½-inch bits

1 packed teaspoon grated fresh ginger, plus more to taste

2 large ripe bananas

½ cup chopped walnuts, toasted

Swish the quinoa in several bowlfuls of fresh water until the water remains fairly clear. Drain in a fine strainer.

Bring the quinoa and 2½ cups of water to a boil in a heavy 3-quart saucepan. Reduce the heat, cover, and simmer until the water has been absorbed, 12 to 15 minutes.

Add the coconut milk, sugar, and salt. Boil gently, uncovered, stirring occasionally, for 5 minutes. Add the mango and ginger. Continue cooking until the mixture thickens to a pudding consistency and the mango is soft but still chewy, about 3 minutes.

Slice half a banana and set aside. Mash the remaining 1½ bananas and, off the heat, stir into the pudding. Add more sugar, if needed, and then stir in the walnuts.

Serve in individual ramekins or from one large bowl, garnished with the banana slices.

OTHER IDEAS

• Sweeten to taste with maple syrup or honey instead of sugar.
• Use raisins or dried pineapple instead of dried mango.
• Instead of walnuts, try Brazil nuts.
• Serve with a scoop of mango or coconut sorbet.
• Garnish with toasted, sweetened coconut flakes.
• Top with slices of fresh mango instead of banana.

baked oatmeal pudding

Here is an elegant way to dress up oatmeal and serve it as a homey, comforting dessert—kind of the way many of us think of rice pudding.

SERVES 8

---

3 ripe bananas

1 cup oatmeal (old-fashioned rolled oats)

¼ teaspoon salt

2 large eggs

1½ cups 2% milk

1 cup chunky applesauce or grated apple

¼ to ⅓ cup (packed) brown sugar, to taste, plus
    2 tablespoons for serving

⅓ cup dried cherries

1 teaspoon vanilla extract

1 teaspoon ground cinnamon

½ teaspoon pumpkin pie spice or ground ginger

2 tablespoons unsalted butter, plus more for
    preparing the pan

½ cup pecan halves

Set a rack in the middle of the oven and preheat the oven to 350°F. Butter a 9 x 9-inch square baking pan. Slice the bananas and layer them on the bottom.

In a heavy 3-quart ovenproof pot, bring 1 cup of water to a boil. Stir in the oatmeal and salt. Cover, turn off the heat, and let sit for 5 minutes.

Meanwhile, beat the eggs in a large bowl. Stir in the milk, applesauce, ¼ cup brown sugar (or more if you like very sweet desserts), dried cherries, vanilla, cinnamon, and pumpkin pie spice.

When the oatmeal has steeped for 5 minutes, stir in the butter. Stir the oatmeal into the egg mixture. Pour over the bananas.

Bake for 25 minutes. Scatter the pecans on top and sprinkle the 2 tablespoons brown sugar over them. Continue baking until the center is set, 25 to 35 minutes longer. Cool on a rack for 10 minutes. Spoon into bowls and serve hot.

versatile mix for cookies, crumbles, and pie crust

With this mix on hand, you can make cookies, fruit crumbles, and pie crusts on a whim. The combination of nuts, whole wheat, and oat flours creates a very forgiving dough, and the recipes using the mix are quite easy: even novice bakers are guaranteed success.

From one batch of Versatile Mix, you'll be able to make four batches of cookies or three batches of cookies plus one fruit crumble and one pie crust—or other combinations, as you choose. I can assure you that no one will guess that these delightful goodies are made with whole-grain flours!

MAKES ABOUT 12½ CUPS

3 cups oatmeal (old-fashioned rolled oats)

2½ cups (packed) dark brown sugar

1¾ teaspoons salt

3½ cups walnuts (13 ounces), or see Other Ideas on page 190)

5 cups whole-wheat pastry flour

Place the oatmeal in the bowl of a food processor fitted with a steel blade and process to a coarse oat flour, about 1 minute. Add the brown sugar and salt, and process 1 minute more. Transfer the mixture to an extra-large (2-gallon) zipper-top plastic freezer bag.

Place the nuts in the processor with 1 cup of the whole-wheat pastry flour. (Do this in two batches if your processor bowl is small.) Pulse until the nuts are fairly finely ground, 30 to 40 seconds. (Do not overprocess or mixture may turn pasty.) Transfer to the plastic bag. Add the remaining flour. Seal the bag, and shake well to distribute the ingredients.

Label and date the bag. Refrigerate or freeze the mix for up to 6 weeks.

peach blueberry crumble

Using the Versatile Mix for the crumble topping makes this homey dessert a snap to prepare—especially if you use frozen, sliced peaches (which are surprisingly sweet and tasty).

Needless to say, the crumble is especially delicious when served warm, with a scoop of vanilla ice cream, a mound of sweetened whipped cream, or a splash of heavy cream on top.

SERVES 8

For the filling

1 pound frozen sliced peaches (4 cups)

12 ounces frozen blueberries (2¼ cups)

Sugar, to taste (optional)

Grated zest of 1 lemon

¼ to ½ teaspoon ground cardamom, to taste

2 tablespoons Versatile Mix (page 187); stir before measuring

For the crumble topping

1¼ cups Versatile Mix (page 187; stir before measuring)

½ teaspoon ground cinnamon

4 tablespoons (½ stick) cold unsalted butter, cut into bits

OTHER IDEAS

• Instead of a pie plate, use an 8-inch square or any other shallow 2-quart baking dish. Increase baking time as needed.

Fresh Fruit Crumble: Use 4 cups sliced soft fruit (1¾ pounds), such as peaches, nectarines, or plums, and 2 cups blueberries, raspberries, or fresh strawberries.

Individual Fruit Crumbles: Bake fruit and crumble toppings in 6 to 8 individual ramekins. Begin checking for doneness after about 20 minutes.

SPEED TIP: Because it's made in a pie plate, this crumble bakes more quickly than a traditional deep-dish baked fruit dessert.

Place a rack in the lower third of the oven and preheat the oven to 400°F. Line a cookie sheet with foil.

Make the filling: Place the peaches and blueberries in a 10-inch pie plate. Toss sugar (if using), lemon zest, cardamom, and 2 tablespoons mix into the fruit.

Prepare the crumble topping: Place the 1¼ cups mix in a bowl. Stir in the cinnamon. With a pastry blender, two knives, or your fingers, work the butter into the flour until the mixture resembles uneven meal. Cover the fruit with the crumble topping.

Set the pie plate on the prepared cookie sheet and bake for 20 minutes.

Raise the oven temperature to 425°F. Rotate the pie plate and bake until the top is lightly browned and the fruit is bubbly, 15 to 20 minutes longer. If the top is well browned before the fruit is bubbly, lightly cover the top with aluminum foil.

Set on a rack to cool for at least 10 minutes. To serve, scoop out portions with a large serving spoon. Serve warm or at room temperature.

orange-scented chocolate chip cookies

Leavened and bound with eggs and enriched with butter, the whole-grain Versatile Mix creates light and puffy cookies that are sturdy to handle, but delicate to eat.

MAKES ABOUT 2½ DOZEN 2-INCH COOKIES

---

3 cups Versatile Mix (page 187)

½ teaspoon baking soda

2 large eggs

12 tablespoons (1½ sticks) unsalted butter, melted and cooled

1½ teaspoons (packed) grated orange zest

1 teaspoon vanilla extract

¾ cup chocolate chips

Place the rack in the middle of the oven and preheat the oven to 375°F. Line one large or two smaller cookie sheets with parchment paper or a silicone baking mat.

Place the mix in a large bowl and stir in the baking soda.

In another bowl, beat the eggs. Blend in the butter, orange zest, and vanilla.

Add the liquid ingredients and chocolate chips to the dry ingredients and stir until well blended.

Drop heaping tablespoons of the batter onto the prepared cookie sheet(s), 2 inches apart. Gently flatten each mound with your fingers or a spatula.

Bake for 5 minutes. Rotate the cookie sheet(s) and continue baking until the bottoms are lightly browned, 4 to 5 minutes more.

Transfer to a cooling rack. Store in an airtight container for up to 3 days, or freeze for up to 3 months.

OTHER IDEAS

Pecan Sandies: Use pecans instead of walnuts in the Versatile Mix. Add coarsely chopped pecans instead of chocolate chips. Press a pecan half into the center of each cookie.

Almond Cookies: Use almonds instead of walnuts in the Versatile Mix and chopped almonds instead of chocolate chips. Add a few drops of almond extract to the liquid ingredients.

Lemon Pignoli Cookies with Rosemary: Use ⅓ cup toasted pine nuts and 2½ packed teaspoons lemon zest instead of the chocolate chips and orange zest. Add 1½ to 2 teaspoons finely chopped fresh rosemary to the liquid ingredients.

versatile pie crust

There is no rolling involved in this easy-to-handle, press-in crust, made from Versatile Mix.

It is prebaked empty and used for puddinglike fillings (see recipes that follow) that require no time in the oven. Its texture is reminiscent of a cookie-crumb crust.

MAKES ONE 10-INCH PIE CRUST

1½ cups Versatile Mix (page 187; stir before measuring)

¼ teaspoon ground cinnamon

4 tablespoons (½ stick) unsalted butter, melted and slightly cooled

SPEED TIP: Make a few crusts at once and freeze them for your own homemade, ready-to-go pies.

Place a rack in the bottom third of the oven and preheat the oven to 400°F.

Combine the mix and cinnamon in a 10-inch pie plate. With a fork, stir in the butter until the flour is completely moistened.

With your fingers or the bottom of a glass, press the dough evenly into the bottom and part way up the sides of the pie plate. Leave the top edge ragged, giving the pie a homespun look, or, if you prefer, even it off with a knife or your fingers.

Bake for 6 minutes. Rotate the pan. Continue baking until the bottom is lightly browned, and the edges are slightly darker, 5 to 7 minutes longer.

Cool on a rack until needed. Alternatively, freeze the cooled crust for up to 2 months. Defrost and recrisp in a 350°F oven before filling.

OTHER IDEAS

• Add the grated zest of 1 large orange to the dry ingredients—especially good with the chocolate filling.
• Add the grated zest of 1 lemon to the dry ingredients when preparing the pie crust.
• Use pumpkin pie spice instead of cinnamon.

chocolate
pudding pie

I have always loved chocolate pudding, and what a treat to have it in a nutty pie crust—the smooth pudding contrasting to the crust's cookielike crunch. A touch of espresso powder intensifies the chocolate flavor.

Cornstarch puddings are so easy to make, I wonder how we all got stuck on instant pudding mix. You'll see what I mean . . .

SERVES 8

⅓ cup sugar

2 tablespoons cornstarch

Pinch of salt

2 cups whole milk

½ cup chopped bittersweet chocolate

1 teaspoon espresso or other instant coffee
   powder (optional)

1 large egg

10-inch prebaked Versatile Pie Crust (page 191)

¼ cup slivered almonds, toasted, for serving

Mix the sugar, cornstarch, and salt in a heavy 2-quart saucepan. Gradually whisk in the milk.

Turn the heat to medium-high. Stir constantly as the mixture comes to a boil and thickens, 8 to 10 minutes. Once you begin to see large bubbles puffing up toward the center, lower the heat to medium, and continue cooking for 1 minute more, stirring occasionally.

Turn the heat to very low. Stir in the chocolate and espresso (if using).

Beat the egg in a small bowl. Whisk a few tablespoons of the hot mixture into the egg. Stir the egg into the pan. Whisk continuously until the pudding thickens further, about 2 minutes. Set the pot on a cooling rack and stir occasionally until the steam subsides.

Pour the filling into the prepared pie shell. After it firms up a bit, sprinkle the almonds on top. Cool to room temperature; then chill until set, at least 2 hours.

OTHER IDEAS
- Add a few drops of mint extract when you add the egg.
- Omit the almonds and garnish with raspberries or sliced strawberries.

butterscotch tapioca pecan pie

I'm somewhat addicted to butterscotch hard candies, but enjoying that luscious flavor in the context of pie is even more addictive.

SERVES 8

2 cups whole milk

2 tablespoons instant tapioca

⅔ cup packed dark brown sugar

5 tablespoons unsalted butter

⅛ teaspoon salt

1 teaspoon vanilla extract

One 10-inch prebaked Versatile Pie Crust
   (page 191)

1 cup pecan halves, toasted

Sweetened whipped cream, for serving
   (optional)

In a 4-cup glass measuring cup, combine the milk and tapioca; set aside for 5 minutes.

Meanwhile, place the brown sugar and butter in a heavy, deep 2-quart saucepan, and set over medium heat. Stir to combine as the butter melts. Cook, stirring frequently, until glossy and bubbly, 4 to 5 minutes. Take care to avoid burning, which can happen in a flash!

Gradually whisk in the tapioca mixture and salt. Turn up the heat to high and stir constantly as you bring the mixture to a full boil. Lower the heat to medium and cook at a gentle boil until the pudding thickens but is still pourable, 5 to 6 minutes.

Turn off the heat. Stir in the vanilla. Pour the mixture into the prepared pie crust. After it firms up a little, about 10 minutes, decoratively arrange the pecans on top. Cool until set, about 1 hour.

Top each portion with whipped cream, if you wish. Or serve whipped cream in a bowl at the table.

banana coconut cream pie

What is it about bananas that make a rich pie filling seem even richer? Perhaps it's their silken texture. Surrounding banana slices by a creamy vanilla pudding accentuates their inherent creaminess.

⅓ cup sugar

¼ cup cornstarch

Pinch of salt

1 can (13.5 ounces) unsweetened coconut milk

Approximately 1⅓ cups milk

1½ teaspoons vanilla extract

2 large ripe, firm bananas

One 10-inch pre-baked Versatile Pie Crust
   (page 191)

Shaved chocolate, for serving (optional)

In a heavy 2-quart saucepan, combine the sugar, cornstarch, and salt.

Empty the can of coconut milk into a 4-cup liquid measuring cup. Add enough milk to equal 3 cups.

With a whisk, blend ½ cup of the coconut milk into the cornstarch mixture until smooth. Blend in the remaining coconut milk.

Set over medium heat and cook just below boiling point, stirring frequently, until the mixture begins to thicken, about 5 minutes. Reduce the heat to low and simmer, stirring constantly, until the mixture develops a puddinglike consistency, 1 to 2 more minutes. Remove from the heat. Stir in the vanilla.

Peel and slice the bananas. Set half the slices on the prepared pie crust and then pour in half the filling. Distribute the remaining bananas over the filling and pour on the remaining filling. Set on a cooling rack in a cool place until set, about 30 minutes.

Garnish with shaved chocolate, if you wish. Serve at room temperature or chilled.

OTHER IDEAS

• Instead of bananas, use sliced mango or papaya.
• Rather than garnishing with chocolate, use toasted sweetened coconut flakes.

fresh fruit—
topped cake mix

Once you've made this mix, with very little effort you can bake a variety of gorgeous cakes that showcase seasonal fruits.

MAKES 4½ CUPS MIX, ENOUGH FOR

THREE 8- OR 9-INCH CAKES

3 cups whole-wheat pastry flour or white
    whole-wheat flour

1½ cups sugar

1 tablespoon baking powder

1 teaspoon baking soda

1 teaspoon salt

1 teaspoon ground cinnamon

Combine the ingredients in a 1-gallon zipper-top bag. Seal the bag and stir or shake well to distribute the ingredients. Label and date the bag. Refrigerate or freeze for up to 3 months.

fresh fruit–topped cake

In this simple recipe, a shallow cake acts as the platform to showcase halved or sliced seasonal fruits. It's very pretty, as you can see from the picture in the photo insert. As the cake rises, the dough puffs up to frame the fruit. You can serve the cake warm from the oven, or at room temperature.

For the tastiest results, select fruits that are ripe, sweet, and juicy, but still firm.

SERVES 6 TO 8

1 large egg

½ to ⅔ cup well-shaken buttermilk

2 tablespoons (¼ stick) unsalted butter, melted, plus more for preparing the pan

Grated zest of 1 large lemon

1½ cups Fresh Fruit–Topped Cake Mix (page 193; stir before measuring)

Choose one of the following:

6 to 8 apricots, halved and pitted

4 large plums, halved, pitted, and sliced

3 medium nectarines, halved and pitted

2 medium peaches, halved and sliced

2 large pears, such as Anjou or Bartlett, cored and sliced

1 large juicy apple, such as Golden Delicious or McIntosh, cored and sliced

1 tablespoon sugar

¼ teaspoon ground cinnamon

OTHER IDEAS

• Instead of melted butter use a nut oil, such as walnut or hazelnut.

• Serve cakes topped with summer fruit warm with a scoop of coconut sorbet on top; serve winter fruit cakes with a scoop of vanilla or butter pecan ice cream.

• Use a 9-inch square pan instead of a round cake pan. Start checking for doneness after 10 minutes. After cooling, cut into 9 squares.

• For a prettier presentation, release the cake from the pan (after it has cooled for a few minutes) by running a knife around the edges. Then flip it out onto a platter and use a second platter to flip it right side up.

SPEED TIP: There is no need to peel any of the fruit.

Set a rack in the middle of the oven and preheat the oven to 375°F. Butter an 8- or 9-inch cake pan. Set aside.

In a medium bowl, lightly beat the egg. Blend in ½ cup of the buttermilk. Then add the melted butter and lemon zest. (It's fine if the mixture curdles.) With a wooden spoon, stir in the cake mix just until most of the flour is absorbed. The mixture should resemble a soft (but not sticky) dough. If it is dry, stir in the extra buttermilk, but do not overmix.

Transfer the dough to the prepared pan and pat it into a thin layer. If necessary, spin the pan on the counter and tap it gently up and down to level the dough a little more.

Evenly distribute the fruit on top: Place the halved summer fruit cut side up. If you feel like fussing, arrange the apple or pear slices in concentric circles; otherwise just distribute them in one layer.

In a small bowl, combine the sugar and cinnamon. Sprinkle over the top.

Bake for 12 minutes. Rotate the pan. Continue baking until a cake tester inserted into the center comes out clean and the top is browned around the edges, 10 to 12 minutes longer. Serve warm or cool on a rack and serve at room temperature.

acknowledgments

WHILE WRITING A BOOK one is constantly reminded that the help of others not only produces better results but is necessary and consoling.

First I would like thank Rica Allannic, editor extraordinaire at Clarkson Potter, for suggesting this idea as the ideal follow-up to *Whole Grains Every Day, Every Way*. It has been a welcome challenge.

Also at Clarkson Potter, my sincere thanks go to Ashley Phillips for doing so many behind-the-scenes essentials, to senior designer Maggie Hinders for producing such a handsome book, and to senior production editor Tricia Wygal.

There are no words to express the abundance of gratitude I feel toward Cathy Roberts who, though she lives far way, has been with me almost every step of the way. Cathy continues to maintain her record of testing every recipe before it is published, pointing out any weak spots, making valuable suggestions for improvement, and cheering me up with cartoons and e-mail pep talks.

Thanks to Kim Pomponi and Amy Quazza of the Institute of Culinary Education in New York City, I have had the company of many enthusiastic and knowledgeable graduates and students for recipe development sessions. They include Cressida Baccay, Danya Bader-Natal, Joseph Baker, Kelly Benedict, Mark deGeorge, Naxielly Dominguez, Debbi Gaspardi, Michelle Gerberino, Carolyn Halyalkar, Barbara Jacobs, Suzanne Lenzer, Ashley Moore, Melissa Radler, Amanda Mayer Robbins, Jeff Seligman, Elizabeth Simms, Christina Simons, Elizabeth Tarpy, Lourdes Taveras, and Barbara Werner. Special thanks to Sukran Demeril, who appeared toward the end of the project and kept coming back, bringing with her the wisdom of the Turkish kitchen and many years of restaurant cooking experience.

Sharon Wooster, president of the Personal Chefs Network, offered to scout out members who might like to help. Those who came on board to retest recipes and offer their insights include Patti Anastasia, Sandy Hall, Jan Harding, Renee Hatch, Cheryl Jagoda, Lance Lemke, Kate Marcus, Leigh Ochs, Megan Lapari Rasmussen, and Edna Rodriguez.

Dedicated home cooks Carrie Feinstein, Susan Freeman, Barbara Lilliston, Cindy Sparks, and Rita Yaezel also generously shared insightful comments after retesting recipes.

Thanks to my dear friends and colleagues who offered ongoing support and understanding along the way, including Jane Assimacopoulos, Michela Biasutti, Judy Bloom, Joyce Curwin, Erin Elliot, Maria Emmer-Aanes, Susan Nobel, and Elizabeth Schneider. A+ neighbor and computer guru Raffaella Depero generously came to my aid on many occasions.

And to Michael Steinman, to whom this book is dedicated, I say, "Thank you, sweetie, for effecting the transformation of a grain goddess into a lucky, happy woman."

mail-order sources

www.bobsredmill.com

(800) 349-2173

Wide range of organic and nonorganic whole grains, grits, and flours. The quinoa distributed under their label is especially good.

www.goldminenaturalfoods.com

(800) 475-FOOD

Organic grains and more, hand-selected by owner, Jean Richardson

www.heirloomrice.com

Heirloom brown and red rices grown by traditional methods on ancient terraces in the Philippines

www.importfood.com

(888) 352-3451

Thai black sticky rice

www.kingarthurflour.com

(802) 649-3361

Barley flakes and whole-grain flours

www.localharvest.org/store/dried-goods.jsp

(No telephone orders)

Heirloom whole-grain corn meal from Salamander Springs Farm in Kentucky—and many more heirloom, organic products from around the country.

www.lotusfoods.com

(866) 972-6879

A variety of heirloom rices, including Chinese Forbidden black, kalijera, and jasmine brown

www.manicaretti.com

(888) 952-4005

Distributors of imported Italian semi-pearled farro and Rustichella d'Abruzzo farro pasta

www.sunnylandmills.com

(559) 233-4983

Organic wheat and Kamut bulgur in four different grinds

index